Foundation History

THE MAKING OF THE UNITED KINGDOM

Patricia Kennedy

Heinemann

Heinemann Library,
an imprint of Heinemann Educational Books Ltd,
Halley Court, Jordan Hill, Oxford OX2 8EJ

OXFORD LONDON EDINBURGH MADRID
ATHENS BOLOGNA PARIS MELBOURNE
SYDNEY AUCKLAND SINGAPORE TOKYO
IBADAN NAIROBI HARARE GABORONE
PORTSMOUTH NH (USA)

First published 1994; this edition 1995

British Library Cataloguing in Publication Data is available from the British Library on request.

ISBN 0-431-06798-8 (Hardback)

Designed by Ron Kamen, Green Door Design Ltd, Basingstoke

Illustrated by Phill Burrows, Jeff Edwards, Peter Hicks and Adam Hook

Printed in China

The front cover shows a detail from the 'Tichborne Dole', painted in 1670 by Giles von Tillborch.

Acknowledgements

The author and publisher would like to thank the following for permission to reproduce photographs:

Achievements Ltd: 5.3A
Bridgeman Art Library: Cover, 2.4A, 2.5A, 4.2A, 4.4G, p.59
British Library: 4.2B, 4.4A, 4.4H
J. Allan Cash Ltd: 3.4C, 4.6B, 5.6B
Professor Rex Cathcart: 5.1A
Viscount De L'Isle (private collection): 2.3A
Edifice/Gillian Darley: 3.4D
Mary Evans Picture Library: 4.1B
Fotomas Index: 1.3A, 3.2D, 3.3H, 4.2G, 4.5H, 5.6A
Hulton Picture Company: 1.3D, 4.1C, 4.2C
Ironbridge Gorge Museum: p.59
Mansell Collection: 1.2A, 2.2B, 3.1C, 3.3A, 3.4A, 4.1A, 4.5B, 5.5C
Museum of London: 4.5A, 4.5G
National Galleries of Scotland: 2.4B
Ann Ronan Picture Library: 4.6A, p.58
Earl of Rosebery: 4.3A
Royal Collection, St. James's Palace © Her Majesty the Queen: 2.2A, 4.2D, 4.2F, 5.2A
Royal Collection, Windsor Castle © Her Majesty the Queen: 1.2E
Shakespeare Birthplace Trust: 3.3E
Joan Shuter: p.59
Weidenfeld & Nicolson Archives: 1.2D
Woodmansterne: 3.3C, 3.4B
Yale Center for British Art, Paul Mellon Collection: 5.5A

Every effort has been made to contact copyright holders of material reproduced in this book. Any omissions will be rectified in subsequent printings if notice is given to the publisher.

Details of written sources

In some sources the wording or sentence structure has been simplified to ensure that the source is accessible.

Thomas Beard, 'The Theatre of God's Judgement', 1597. In: D. Underdown, *Revel Riot and Rebellion*, OUP, 1987: 1.2B
'The Book of Common Prayer', 1559. In: *History Today*, March, 1984: 1.2C
Hugh Brogan, *Pelican History of the USA*, Pelican, 1986: 5.3C
Daniel Defoe, *Journey Through the Whole of Great Britain, 1724* (Ed. Pat Rogers), Penguin, 1971: 5.5D
Celia Fiennes, *The Journeys of Celia Fiennes* (Ed. C. Morris), London, 1947: 5.5B
C. H. Firth, *Clarke Papers*, Camden Society, 1891: 4.4D, 4.4F
S. R. Gardiner, *Constitutional Documents of the Puritan Revolution*, OUP, 1906: 4.4C
J. Gilingham, 'The Origins of English Imperialism'. In: *History Today*, February, 1987: 3.3G
Glossop Parish Overseer's Accounts, 1686, Derbyshire Records Office: 3.2C
William Harrison, 'Description of England', 1587. In: J. Dover Wilson, *Life in Shakespeare's England*, Penguin, 1944: 3.1A, 3.1B, 3.1E
Bishop Jewel, 'Zurich Letters', 1559. In: Thomas, 1973: 1.3B
R. McCrum, *The Story of English*, BBC Books, 1986: 3.3F
Sir Thomas More, 'Utopia', 1516. In: N. L. Frazer, *English History Illustrated from Original Sources, 1485–1603*, Black, 1908: 3.2A
J. E. Neale, *Queen Elizabeth I*, Penguin, 1960: 2.2B, 2.3B, 2.4C
Samuel Pepys, *Diary*, (Eds. R. Latham, W. Mathews Bell), 1970: 4.5C, 4.5D, 4.5E, 4.5F
G. W. Prothero, *Select Statutes and Constitutional Documents, 1559–1625*, OUP, 1913: 2.3C, 3.2B, 4.2E
Paul Shuter, John Child, *Skills in History 2*, Heinemann Educational, 1989: 4.4B, 4.4E
John Stow, 'Annals', 1605. In: Joe Scott, *Energy Through Time*, OUP, 1986: 3.1D
Keith Thomas, *Religion and the Decline of Witchcraft*, Penguin, 1973: 1.3C
F. J. Weaver, *English History Illustrated from Original Sources, 1603–1660*, Black, 1908: 5.3B
William Whately, 'The Bridal Bush', London, 1617. In: L. Stone, *The Family, Sex and Marriage in England 1500–1800*, Penguin, 1979: 1.2F

95 96 97 98 10 9 8 7 6 5 4 3 2 1

CONTENTS

1.1 Disunited Kingdoms

Britain in 1500

In 1500, the King of England was Henry VII. Henry also ruled Wales and part of Ireland. Scotland was a country with its own king.

Language

People in England and Wales did not all speak English. People in Ireland did not all speak English. You can see the different languages people spoke on the map on this page.

Changes

But things were changing. Between 1500 and 1750, Britain became stronger and richer. The different parts of the British Isles were brought closer together.

One reason for this was that the design of ships got better. This meant it was easier to sail to any part of Britain.

There were other reasons why Britain was changing. This book will look into them.

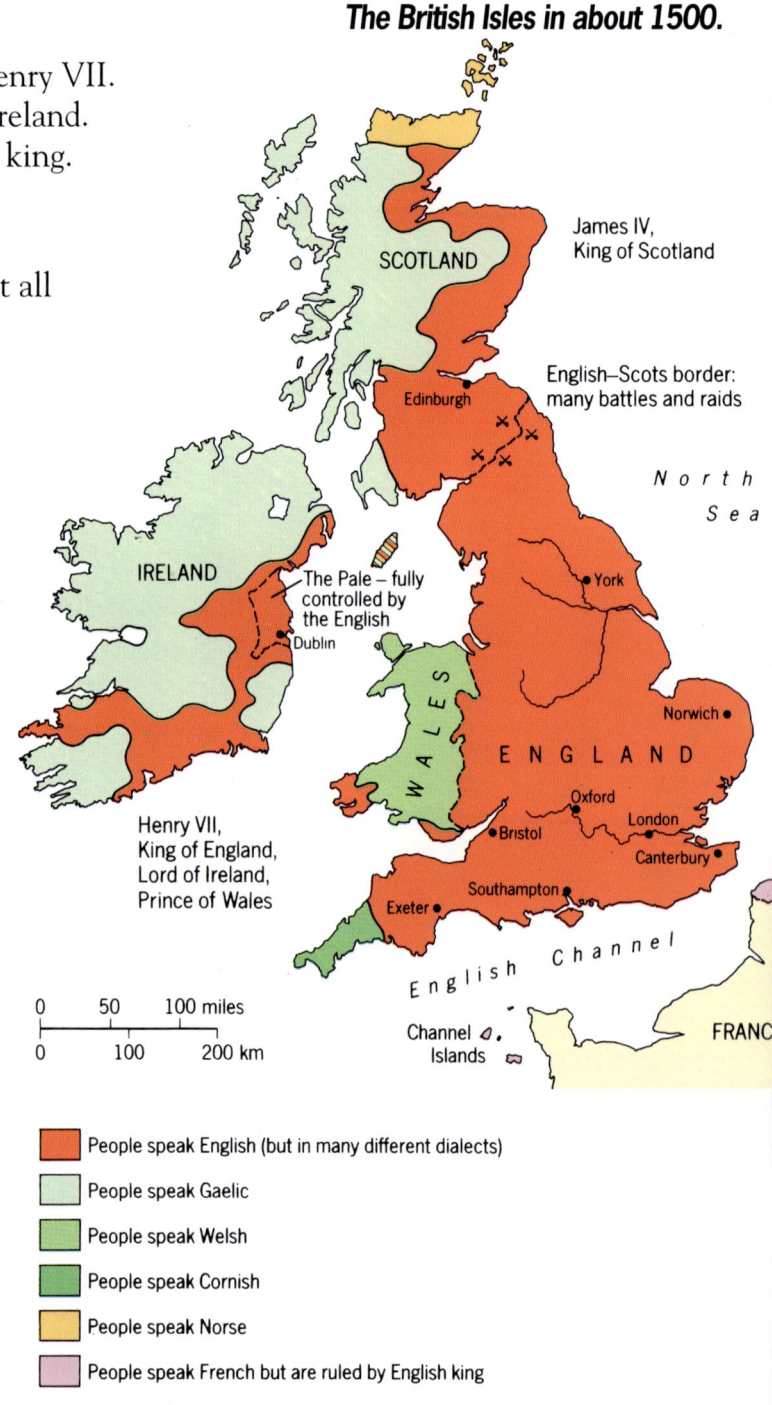

The British Isles in about 1500.

James IV, King of Scotland

SCOTLAND

Edinburgh

English–Scots border: many battles and raids

North Sea

IRELAND

The Pale – fully controlled by the English

Dublin

York

W A L E S

E N G L A N D

Norwich

Oxford

London

Bristol

Canterbury

Henry VII, King of England, Lord of Ireland, Prince of Wales

Exeter

Southampton

English Channel

0   50   100 miles
0   100   200 km

Channel Islands

FRANC

■ People speak English (but in many different dialects)

■ People speak Gaelic

■ People speak Welsh

■ People speak Cornish

■ People speak Norse

■ People speak French but are ruled by English king

● Towns with over 5,000 people

✕ Battles

Henry VII

Henry VII (1457–1509). The families of Lancaster and York fought over who ruled England. Henry, a Lancastrian, beat the Yorkist king Richard III in 1485, then married Elizabeth of York.

1.2 Lords and Masters

The monarch and the people.

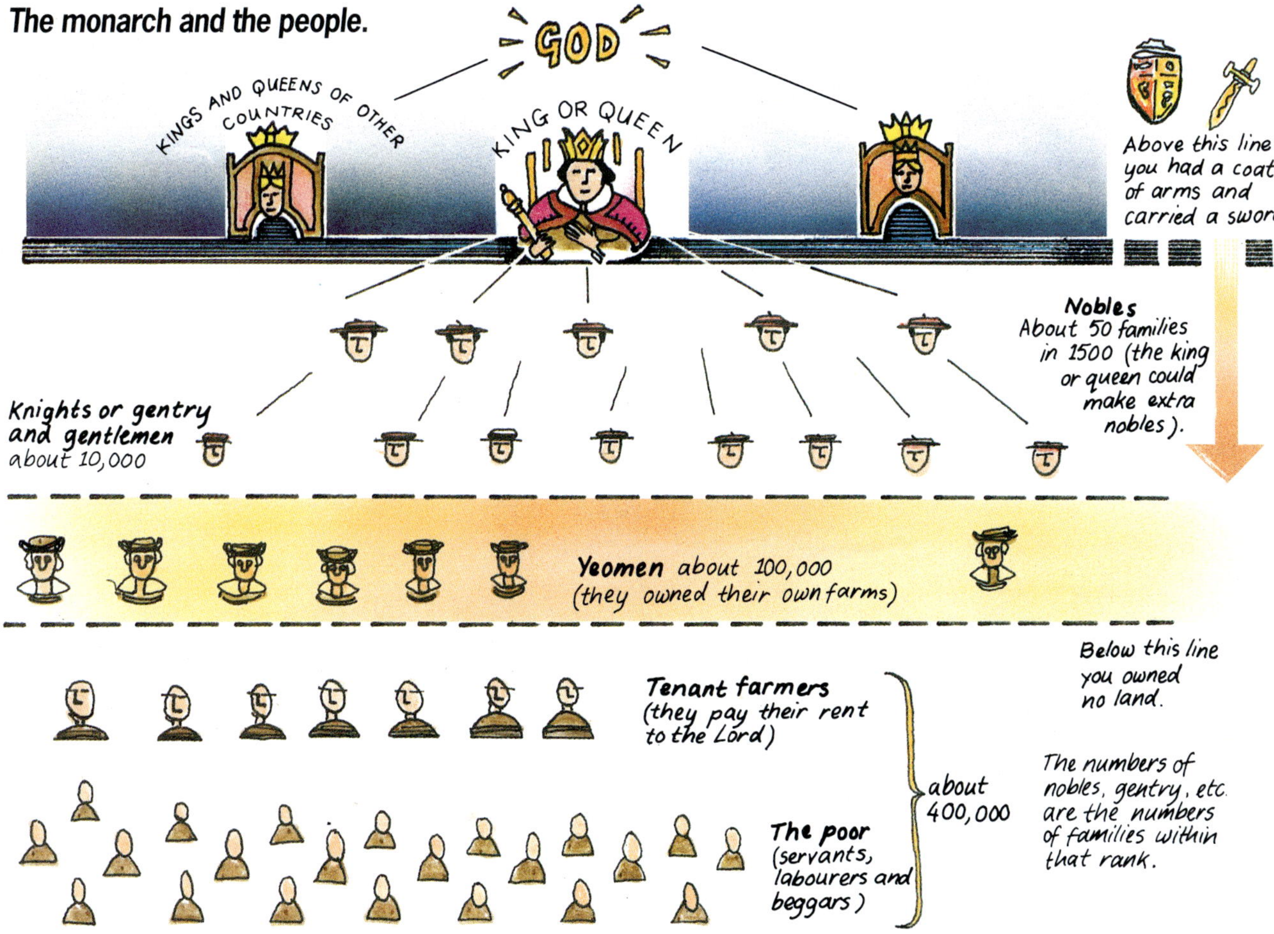

GOD

KINGS AND QUEENS OF OTHER COUNTRIES

KING OR QUEEN

Above this line you had a coat of arms and carried a sword.

Nobles
About 50 families in 1500 (the king or queen could make extra nobles).

Knights or gentry and gentlemen
about 10,000

Yeomen *about 100,000 (they owned their own farms)*

Below this line you owned no land.

Tenant farmers *(they pay their rent to the Lord)*

about 400,000

The poor *(servants, labourers and beggars)*

The numbers of nobles, gentry, etc. are the numbers of families within that rank.

Look at the diagram above. In 1500, everyone in England had someone above them. Even the monarch (the king or queen) had someone above them – God!

Everyone knew his or her place in this order. People accepted their places, and did not try and move out of them. People thought it was important to marry people at the same level, or higher.

The person above you was supposed to be kind and helpful to you. You were supposed to obey and respect the person above you. Even in families, wives and children had to show respect for the head of the family.

Of course, some people might have broken these rules.

In 1500 there were about 2¼ million (2,250,000) people in England. Everyone belonged to a level or rank. A wife had the same rank as her husband.

Rules of rank

Only people of lower ranks were whipped or branded.

Only gentlemen carried swords.

The village

LORD OF THE MANOR. Ran the manor court which settled problems in the village.

Everyone used the common land for animals and firewood.

RICH YEOMEN – owned their own land.

TENANT FARMERS – Rented the lord's land.

THE POOR – No Land.

In 1500, 9 out of 10 people lived in villages of 500 people or less.

Parliament

Parliament was made up of two parts, or 'houses'. Members of the House of Lords were nobles and bishops. Members of the House of Commons were elected. Each county and important town could elect two Members of Parliament (MPs).

What did Parliament do?

Parliament let the monarch know what people in the country thought. Also, Parliament had some control over money. For example, the monarch might need more money to fight a war. Parliament could vote for extra taxes to get the money for the monarch.

A SOURCE

A tenant paying his rent in 1523.

D SOURCE

A picture of an execution in 1552. Nobles had their heads chopped off.

Parliament in 1523. Members of the House of Lords are sitting. Members of the House of Commons are standing at the back on the right.

A good wife should think: 'My husband has authority over me. Nature and God have given it to him.'

Written by William Whateley, a clergyman, in 1617.

Rewards

Monarchs tried to keep the nobles and gentry on their side. So they gave them rewards and special jobs. Some nobles were made generals in the army. Some of the gentry were made Justices of the Peace (JPs). JPs helped to run the part of the country they lived in.

The court

The people who lived in the same place as the monarch were called the court. These people helped to run the monarch's life, and helped to run the country.

In the summer the court moved around the country. People came to watch the processions and parties of the court. This made the monarch popular.

Henry VIII

Henry VIII (1491–1547) was just eighteen years old when he became king. Henry was big and handsome as a young man. He enjoyed sport and music.

But Henry was also ruthless. He often executed his opponents. He wanted to be more powerful. Parliament helped him to become Head of the Church in England, instead of the Pope.

Henry was married six times.

1.3 The Church

God and the Devil

Everybody believed in God. People believed that God made everything and looked after it. People also believed in the Devil, who was evil. They believed that if you obeyed God, you went to Heaven when you died. If you did not obey God, you went to Hell.

People tried to explain things they did not understand by saying that God or the Devil had caused them. People also believed in angels and ghosts, witches and demons.

The Church

'The Church' does not just mean the building where people worshipped God. The Church was the whole organization that ran the lives of Christians.

At the head of the Church was the Pope, who lived in Rome. Under the Pope were the archbishops. Under the archbishops were the bishops.

What did the Church do?

The Church was very powerful. The bishops and archbishops helped the monarch to rule. The Church was also very rich. It owned about one third of all the land in England. It also ran the universities and helped the poor.

The local church

Everyone in a village helped to pay for the local church. The church was used for things like christenings, marriages and funerals. People believed that the priest was the link between them and God.

This drawing was made in 1579. God is at the top, in Heaven. The Devil is at the bottom, in Hell. Between them are angels, saints, people, birds, fish, animals and plants.

B The number of witches has become very large.

This was said by an English bishop in 1559.

C Everywhere in the land is full of witches.

This was said by an English judge in 1602.

Life for most people in 1500 was very short. Why?

1 There were many accidents.
2 There were more diseases, and fewer cures for them.
3 If the harvest was bad, there was not enough food to go round.
4 Many women died having babies.

Because life was short for many people, they wanted to believe in a life after death. So the Church was very important to them.

This picture shows a witch, a demon and a warlock. It was made in the 1500s.

Church organization

The Pope was Head of the Roman Catholic Church. He was more important than anyone but God. A Pope ruled until he died.

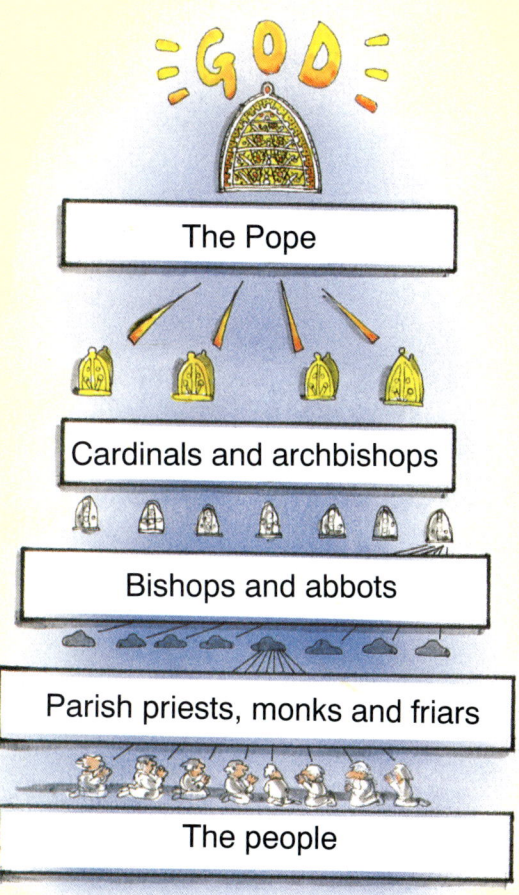

The Pope

Cardinals and archbishops

Bishops and abbots

Parish priests, monks and friars

The people

The Church

Thomas Wolsey

Thomas Wolsey (1475–1529) was a priest who worked for Henry VIII. He was very loyal and Henry rewarded him by giving him jobs and power.

Wolsey did a lot of the day-to-day running of the country for the king. Until 1525 he was very successful. Then Henry decided he wanted a divorce. He could only have a divorce if the Pope gave permission. Wolsey tried but failed to arrange a divorce for Henry.

Wolsey's enemies accused him of treason. In 1529 Henry called him to answer the charges. Wolsey died on the way to London.

2.1 Henry VIII Takes Control of the Church

What was Henry VIII like?

When Henry VIII was young he was strong and handsome. He was clever and liked to have his own way.

Henry VIII and family problems

Henry and his first wife, Catherine, had lots of babies. But only one of the babies lived, a girl called Mary. Henry wanted a son to rule after him. But Catherine could not have any more babies, so Henry wanted to divorce her. He was now in love with Anne Boleyn, and wanted to marry her. Catholics needed the Pope to agree to let them divorce. The Pope refused.

The divorce

In 1533, Anne Boleyn was pregnant. If the baby was a boy it could be the next king. Henry wanted to marry Anne before the baby was born. He got the Archbishop of Canterbury to give him a divorce. The Pope was not pleased.

Head of the Church

In 1534, Parliament made Henry the Head of the Church in England. Henry had broken away from the Catholic Church, and he did not have to answer to the Pope. Henry now had much more power. But he also needed more money. The Church was very rich, and the monasteries had some of the best land in England. Henry closed down the monasteries and took their land.

Henry VIII and the Protestant Church

Henry did not like the Protestant Church. But his quarrel with the Pope meant that many English people became Protestants. Henry tried to stop them, but failed.

A

SOURCE

A painting of Henry VIII. Henry actually posed for this painting.

B

SOURCE

Sir Thomas More. More was a friend of Henry VIII, and helped him run the country. But he would not accept Henry as Head of the Church. He was executed.

Protestants and Catholics

Until this time, there had been only one way to worship the Christian God. That was in the **Catholic Church**.

In Germany, a monk called **Martin Luther** thought that the Catholic Church was worshipping God in the wrong way. Luther said that people had to understand church services. So church services should be in your own language, not Latin. He also said the Pope should not run the Church in every country. Luther wanted the Catholic Church to change. The Pope disagreed.

Luther and his followers were called **Protestants**. They caused a split in the Catholic Church. Now there were two groups believing in God – Catholics and Protestants.

The Tudor monarchs.

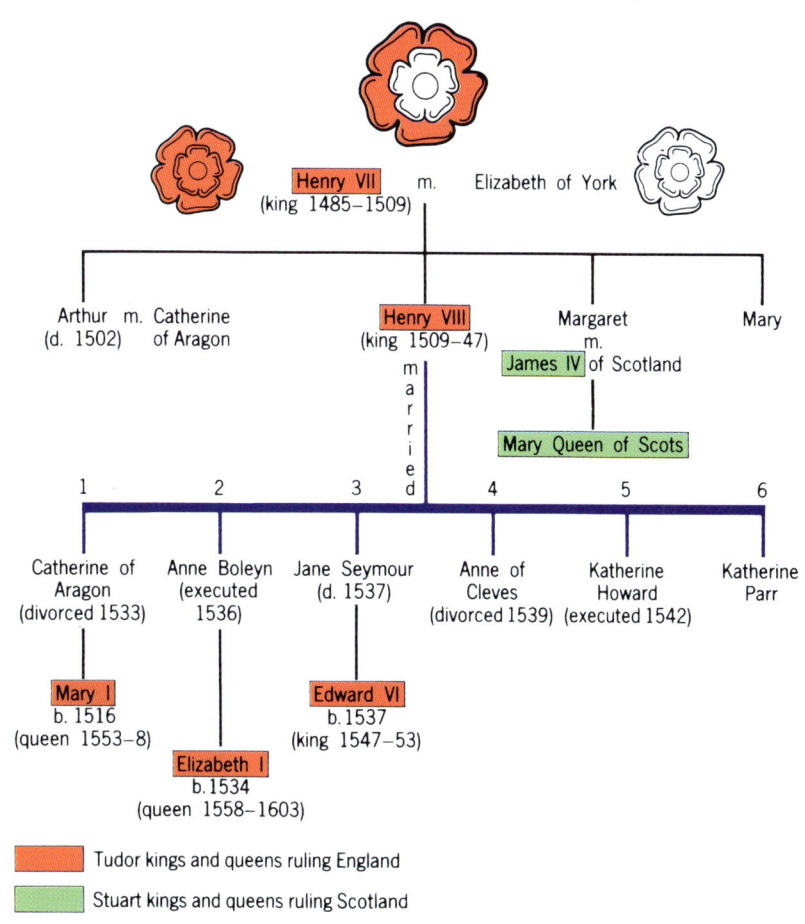

Tudor kings and queens ruling England

Stuart kings and queens ruling Scotland

Sir Thomas More

Sir Thomas More (1478–1535) trained as a lawyer. Henry VIII liked him, and knighted him. He also made him Lord Chancellor in 1529.

More wrote a lot of books, including one in which he said people should be kinder to the poor. He was interested in new ideas, but disagreed with the new Protestant ideas about religion. He thought the Pope should be Head of the Church.

In 1532 Henry, who wanted a divorce that the Pope would not give him, decided to make himself Head of the English Church. More thought this was wrong. He resigned in protest.

Henry had Parliament pass a law that made it treason for anyone not to agree that he was Head of the Church. More refused. The king accused him of treason. More was executed for treason in 1535.

2.2 The Tudors in Trouble

Edward VI

Henry VIII died in 1547. His son, Edward, became king. He was only nine years old. But how could a little boy rule like a king? His uncle, the Duke of Somerset, took control until 1551. He called himself Lord Protector. From 1551–53, the Duke of Northumberland took his place.

The Church

Both of the Protectors were Protestants. So Edward was brought up as a Protestant too. They brought in a new prayer book with Protestant services. The prayer book was in English, not Latin. Parliament ordered every church to use the new prayer book. Many people did not like these changes.

Problems for Edward

In 1549 there was a rebellion in Cornwall. Protector Somerset sent soldiers to stop the rebellion. The leaders were hanged.

Also in 1549, there was a rebellion in Norfolk. This was caused by the changes in religion, and by other problems. There had been some bad harvests, and people had been turned off their farms.

The bad harvests meant that prices were rising. Look at the graph on the right. The cost of living was going up more than wages were. Poor people were having a bad time.

SOURCE

A

A picture of Edward VI, painted in about 1550.

Wages and prices in England, 1550–1610.

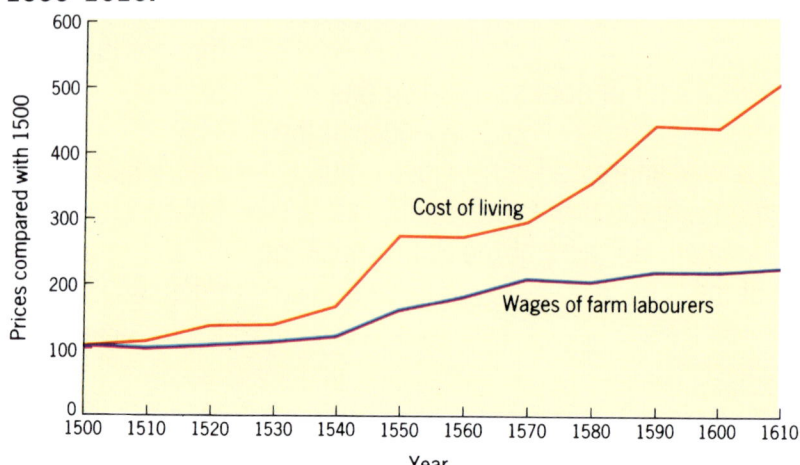

Cost of living

Wages of farm labourers

Prices compared with 1500

Year

Mary I

Edward died in 1553. His sister, Mary, became queen. Mary was a Catholic. She tried to make religion more Catholic again. She brought back Catholic services in church.

The Spanish marriage

In 1554, Mary married Philip, the son of the King of Spain. Spain was the most powerful country in Europe. It was also a very Catholic country. The English were worried that Philip would tell Mary how to run the country. Also, if Philip and Mary had a son he would rule both Spain and England. In 1554, there was a rebellion in Kent against the wedding. Soldiers were sent to stop the rebellion and its leaders were hanged.

Problems with the Protestants

Not everyone was glad to let England become Catholic again. Protestants wanted to keep the new ways of worship. Mary tried to get rid of the Protestants. They were arrested. If they refused to become Catholics they were burned to death. Between 1555 and 1558 over 8,300 Protestants were killed.

Death of Mary

Mary died in 1558. She had no children. Her sister, Elizabeth became queen. Elizabeth was a Protestant.

B

SOURCE

Lord receine my spirit

A picture of Thomas Cranmer, the Protestant Archbishop of Canterbury, being burned for not becoming a Catholic. It comes from a book by John Foxe which was printed in 1559.

Thomas Cranmer

Thomas Cranmer (1489–1556) said Henry VIII did not need the Pope's consent to divorce. In 1532 Henry made Cranmer Archbishop of Canterbury as a reward.

Cranmer believed in the new Protestant ideas. He did not think the Pope should be Head of the Church. He believed that the Bible and Prayer Book should be translated into English. He also believed in allowing clergy to marry. He was married.

When Henry died, his son Edward became king. He wanted more Protestant changes to the English Church. Cranmer agreed.

When Edward died, his Catholic sister Mary became queen. Cranmer was torn between obeying his ruler and following his religious beliefs. Mary arrested him and put him in the Tower of London. He said he would obey her as his ruler. But her Catholic bishops burned him all the same.

2.3 Two Problems for Queen Elizabeth

What was Elizabeth I like?

Elizabeth became queen in 1558. She was twenty-five years old, clever and attractive. Elizabeth listened to people and then made up her own mind about things.

Marriage

People expected Elizabeth to marry. A husband would help her rule the country. She was also expected to have a son, who could be king after her.

"Marry a Protestant"

"Marry a foreign Prince"

"Marry a Catholic."

"Marry a noble Englishman"

Religion

Elizabeth was not a Catholic. She did not follow the very strong Protestant ideas, either. She felt people were tired of all the changes in the way they worshipped.

B

SOURCE

She loves her people and they love her. She gives her orders and has her way just as her father did.

If she decides to marry out of the country she will at once fix her eyes on Your Majesty.

Written by the Spanish Ambassador to Philip II of Spain in 1559.

C

SOURCE

Elizabeth is only the pretended queen of England. I command all people not to obey her orders.

Part of an order sent out by the Pope in 1570 to all Catholics.

A

SOURCE

This picture, painted at the time, may show Elizabeth I dancing.

> We humbly beg that your Majesty may be graciously pleased to marry so that....

Elizabeth tried to find a religion for the country, that would please most people. She used a mixture of old and new ideas.

1 She made herself Head of the Church.
2 Services were in English.
3 Everyone had to go to church.

If Catholics refused to go to church they were fined. But they were not burned or treated badly just because they were Catholics.

The new church was called the Church of England. It pleased many people. They were glad that things had stopped changing. But not everyone was happy.

Catholics

Some people stayed Catholic. In 1570 the Pope said Elizabeth I was not the real ruler of England. He said all Catholics should try to replace her with a Catholic ruler. This was asking English Catholics to be traitors. Parliament made it treason (acting against the monarch) to try to make people become Catholic. Catholic priests who tried to do this were arrested, tortured and executed.

The Puritans

Many strict Protestants wanted plain and simple church services. They said the Church should stop anything that made people sin. This meant stopping things like dancing or going to the theatre. Puritans felt the Church should be run by the men God had chosen – themselves.

The Earl of Leicester

Robert Dudley (about 1532–88), the Earl of Leicester, was the son of a nobleman and went to Queen Elizabeth I's Court. He was tall and handsome. Elizabeth enjoyed his company. They went hunting and dancing together. Some people wondered if she wished that she could marry him.

But Leicester was married already. His wife, Amy, was not welcome at Court. Leicester seldom left court. Amy was found dead at the bottom of the stairs at their home. She had probably killed herself. But many people said Leicester had fixed her murder to be free to marry Elizabeth. All this talk made it impossible for them to marry.

2.4 Mary, Queen of Scots

In 1562, Elizabeth nearly died from smallpox. She was still not married. She had no children to rule after her. This made her ministers think about who would rule England if she died.

Mary, Queen of Scots

Elizabeth's closest relative was the queen of Scotland (see the family tree on page 11). Mary was nine years younger than Elizabeth. But even more important, Mary already had a son, called James.

There were problems with Mary becoming queen.
1   Mary was a Catholic.
2   She had been brought up in France, a Catholic country, which was often at war with England.

Mary leaves Scotland

In 1568, Mary's husband was killed. Many people thought Mary had ordered his murder. The Scots were mainly Protestant, and disliked Mary because she was a Catholic. In 1568, the Scots rebelled. Elizabeth sent soldiers to help the Scots fight Mary. She also sent ships to stop the French helping Mary. Mary lost. She escaped to England and left her son behind. James was made King of Scotland and was brought up as a Protestant.

What to do with Mary?

Elizabeth decided that it would be safest to keep Mary in England, as a prisoner. The Pope said that Mary was the proper ruler of England. Many Catholics wanted Mary as Queen of England. Mary was held prisoner until 1587. Even in prison Mary became part of many plots to make her Queen of England (see box on this page).

A SOURCE

A painting of Mary, Queen of Scots at the age of 17.

Plots

There were many plots to make Mary queen instead of Elizabeth. In some of these plots Philip of Spain promised to help the Catholics. Many people thought that Mary was plotting against Elizabeth, but nobody could prove it.

The Babington plot, 1586

Babington and other Catholics planned to kill Elizabeth and put Mary on the throne. Elizabeth's spies read Babington's letters to Mary. Mary agreed to the plan in her letters. Babington and his friends were arrested. Now Elizabeth had evidence against Mary too.

A painting of the execution of Mary, Queen of Scots in 1587.

The last plot

In 1586, Elizabeth's spies finally proved that Mary had plotted to murder Elizabeth. Mary was put on trial and found guilty. Elizabeth tried everything to avoid signing the death warrant. Mary was a queen – and her cousin! But in the end Elizabeth signed.

Sir Francis Walsingham

Sir Francis Walsingham (about 1530–90) was one of Elizabeth I's chief advisers. He hated and feared Catholics, and thought they were always plotting to replace Elizabeth with a Catholic monarch. They probably were.

Walsingham had a network of spies at home and abroad. He found out about several Catholic plots against the queen. He heard about the Babbington Plot with Mary Queen of Scots. He wanted proof that she knew about the plot. He did not arrest the plotters at once, but watched them. They sent messages in barrels going in and out of the castle Mary was imprisoned in. When he had clear evidence that Mary was involved, he had everyone arrested.

C Better to have poisoned her or smothered her, than to have so public a death.

Said by a Spaniard on hearing of the execution in 1587.

2.5 War with Spain

In 1588, Philip II of Spain tried to invade England. Why did he decide to attack England? Philip decided to attack partly because Mary, Queen of Scots had been executed. He thought the people who had killed a Catholic queen had to be punished. But there were other reasons too.

The Netherlands

Philip ruled the Netherlands, which was a Protestant country. The Netherlands was fighting to be free from Spain. England was helping the Netherlands.

A painting of Elizabeth I, made to celebrate the defeat of the Spanish Armada in 1588.

A map of western Europe in 1588. The red line shows the route that the Spanish Armada took.

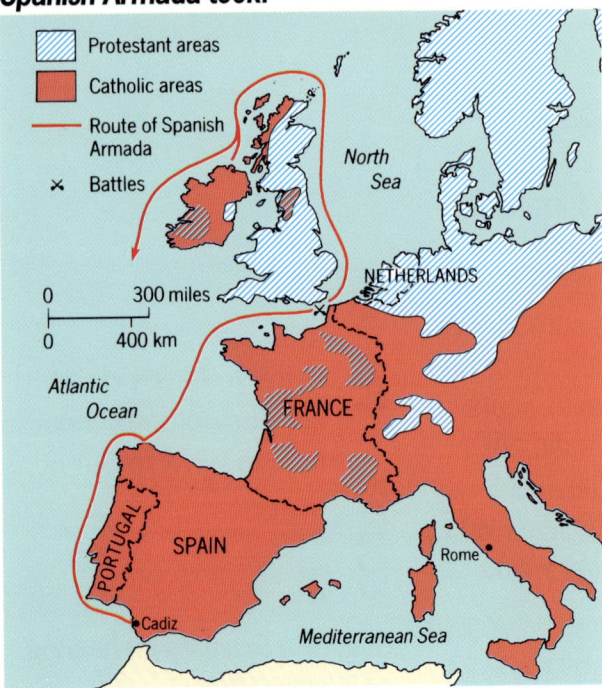

A map of the Atlantic, and North and South America during the reign of Elizabeth I.

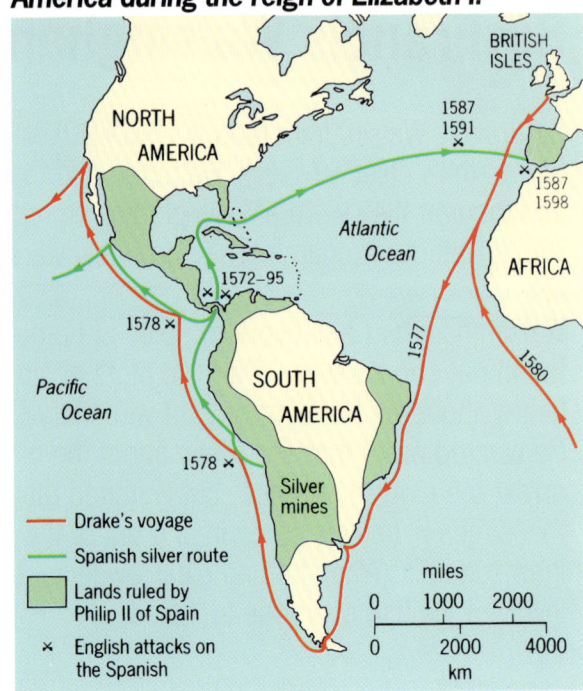

Spanish silver

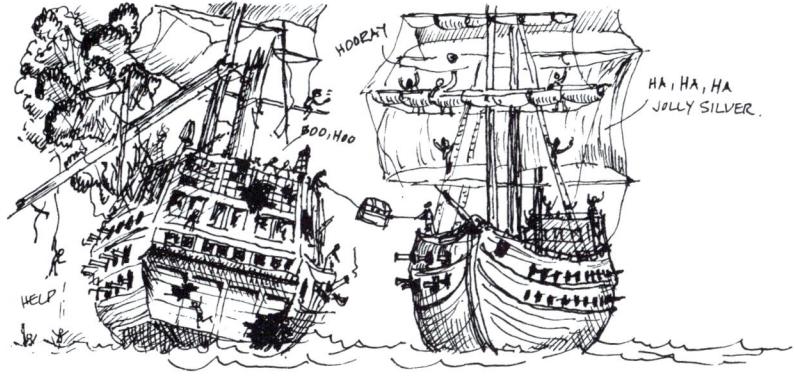

The Sea Dogs

The English sailors who tried to capture Spanish silver were called the 'Sea Dogs'. One of them was Francis Drake. Between 1577 and 1580, Drake sailed around the world. He captured lots of Spanish treasure on the way. He made a lot of money. So did the people who helped to pay for the journey. One of these people was Queen Elizabeth!

The Spanish Armada

The Plan:

Philip had 130 ships and 30,000 men. They were to sail to France, collect 30,000 soldiers, and invade England.

1 The English attacked the Armada while it waited for the extra soldiers.
2 The night after the English attack there was a bad storm. It broke up the Armada, and many ships were wrecked trying to get home.

What happened next?

1 England went on helping the Netherlands.
2 The Netherlands became a separate country.
3 The Spanish went on trying to make England Catholic. They helped some Irish Catholics to fight the English. English ships still attacked Spanish ships.

By 1604 both Elizabeth I and Philip II were dead. The two countries made peace.

Sir Francis Drake

Sir Francis Drake (about 1540–95) was a sailor who traded with Africa and Spanish South America. The Spanish said that the English could not trade with South America. In 1567 some English sailors, heading for South America, were attacked by the Spanish. Many of them were captured. Drake escaped. After this he and his friends often raided Spanish ships. It made him rich and, of course, he gave part of the loot to Elizabeth.

The Spanish complained about the raids of Drake and the other 'Sea Dogs'. Elizabeth did not openly support them. This would lead to war with Spain. But she happily took a share of their loot and knighted several of them, including Drake. He took part in the defeat of the Spanish Armada in 1588.

3.1 England Gets Richer

Trade

In the 1500s, ships from countries like Spain and England sailed to many parts of the world. There was trade in lots of different goods.

Industry

'To export' means to send goods out of a country. England made woollen cloth and exported it to other countries. By 1600, cloth made in England was sold as far away as Russia.

The world known to Europeans in about 1480.

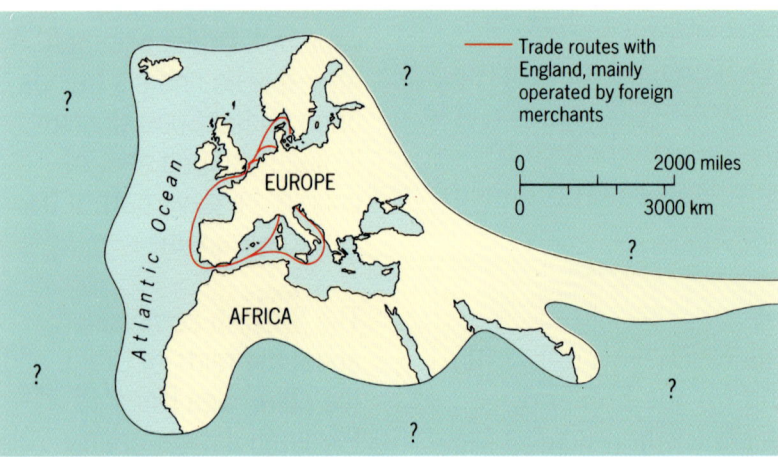

The world known to Europeans by about 1600.

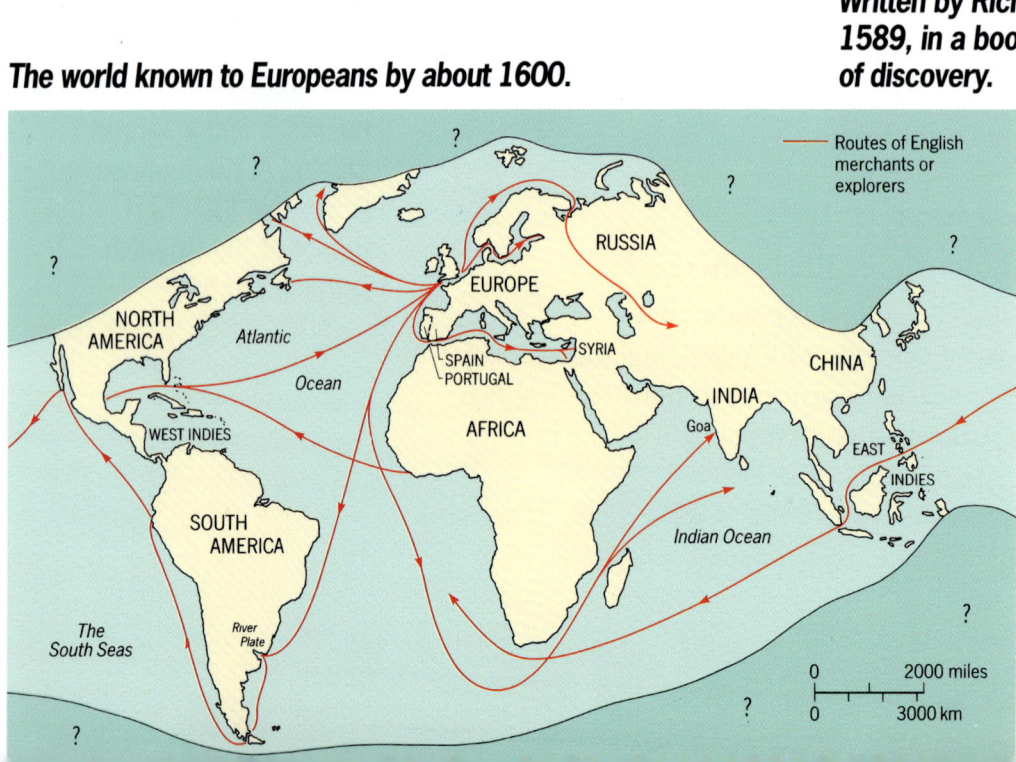

A SOURCE

Foreigners think that our ships are the best in the world for strength, nimbleness and speed.

Written by William Harrison, in 'Description of England', 1577.

B SOURCE

Whoever heard of Englishmen in India before now? No English ships anchored in the mighty Plate [in South America] before now. No English ships crossed the South Seas and returned home with goods from China before now.

Written by Richard Hakluyt in 1589, in a book about journeys of discovery.

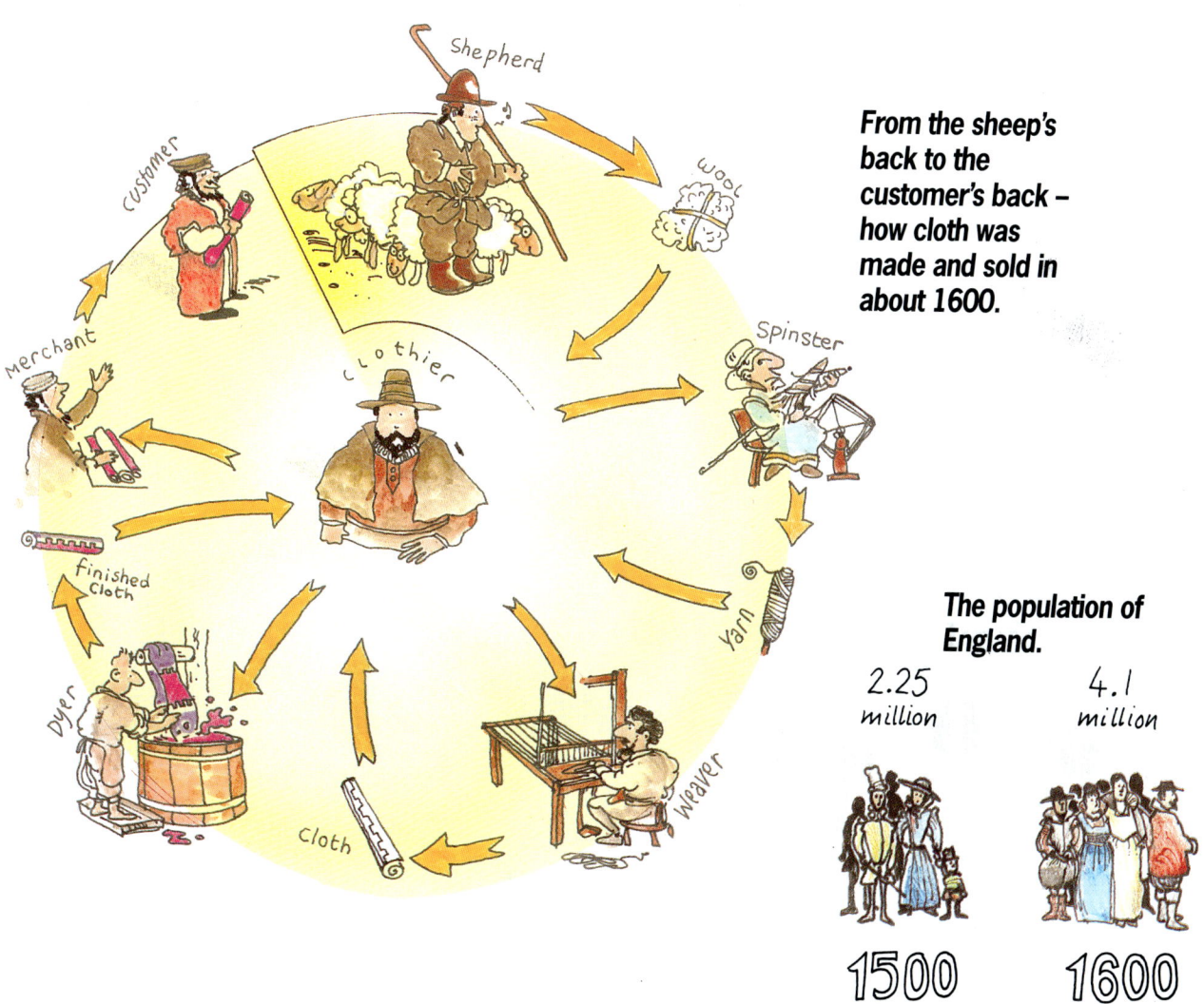

From the sheep's back to the customer's back – how cloth was made and sold in about 1600.

Shepherd
wool
Spinster
Yarn
Weaver
Cloth
Dyer
finished cloth
Merchant
customer
clothier

The population of England.

2.25 million	4.1 million
1500	1600

Anthony Jenkinson

Anthony Jenkinson (about 1525–1611) was a sailor and trader.

In 1557 he was sent to Russia. He was working for a new company that was trying to set up trade links with Russia. It was called the Muscovy Company. It was opening up a new route to Russia. Jenkinson went on the new route, north of Norway. He reached Russia in July. He travelled up the rivers and on sledges until he reached Moscow in December. The Tsar of Russia said he could go further into Russia to set up trade links.

His travels through Russia were dangerous. He was attacked by thieves and local chiefs. His ship was wrecked crossing the Caspian Sea. He then crossed the desert on camels and arrived in Bokhara. This was a trading city for China, India and Persia. When Jenkinson came back, he wrote a detailed description of his trip for the Muscovy Company. Trade links were set up.

Jenkinson married and had seven children who lived to adulthood.

A print of the view looking north across London Bridge, made in the late 1500s.

Peace and wealth

Tudor monarchs like Henry VIII and Elizabeth I brought peace to England. Rebellions were easily stopped. Sometimes England fought other countries, like Spain, but the fighting was not in England. Because England was at peace, it grew rich.

London

Lots of towns grew. London grew the most. In 1500 there were about 50,000 people living in London. By 1660 there were about 200,000 people. It was where most of the trading went on for the whole country. Ships used the River Thames to get to London. Farmers sold their extra food to people in London. New industries (like glassmaking) and old industries (like shipbuilding) both grew. Iron-making in Sussex made cannons for ships and pokers for everyone's fires.

The north of England

There was less change in the north of England. Some industries did grow, like the cloth industry. Coal was taken from here by sea to London. Londoners called it 'sea coal'.

It is difficult to get any wood. Londoners have lately discovered how to make glass and bricks using sea coal.

From 'Annals', by John Stowe, 1605.

London is a mighty city of business. Most men work in trade. Ships from other countries use the river to come up almost to the city.

Written by a German who visited London in 1592.

Sir Thomas Gresham

Sir Thomas Gresham (about 1519–79) was a London merchant. He traded lots of things. He also bought and sold foreign money. He advised Henry VIII, Edward VI, Mary I and Elizabeth I about making money. They paid him for his advice (it worked!). He became very rich.

Thomas Sutton

Thomas Sutton (1532–?) was a soldier. He bought and rented coal mines that supplied coal to London. There were a lot of people in London. They all needed coal. Sutton became very rich. He made more money by lending out money. He became one of the richest men in England.

A **Peace**

B **Trade**

Helps to cause

Helps to cause

C **Growth of industries**

Helps to cause

D **The wool trade**

Helps to cause

MONEY £

Growing wealth for England

3.2 The Poor Get Poorer

Even though some people in England got richer some people got poorer. Why?

1 In the 1500s, food prices went up faster than wages.
2 Some landowners were enclosing land.

Enclosure

Enclosure meant fencing off land that everyone farmed. Some landowners enclosed all the fields around their villages. Some even enclosed the villages. In all these cases, people had to leave their homes. But it wasn't just taking the land that made life difficult for the poor. The landowners often changed from growing crops to keeping sheep. They needed fewer workers to keep sheep, so many people had to leave their homes. It was hard for them to find work anywhere else.

Parliament acts

Parliament passed laws against enclosure. They did not work. The people who were supposed to make the laws work were often the ones doing the enclosing!

The Poor Law, 1601

In 1601, a Poor Law was passed. Money, called a poor rate, was collected. The Poor Law split the poor into three sorts:

1 People who were too old, too young, or too sick to work. These people were given money.
2 'Sturdy beggars' (those who were fit but not working). They were whipped and made to work, or put in prison.
3 Beggars from other villages were whipped and sent home.

How people saw the poor

For the first time in a long time there was not enough work for everyone. Most people were not used to this. They thought that people who were fit to work, but who were not working, were being lazy.

It took people a while to realize that there were more people than jobs.

A

SOURCE

When fields are enclosed the people are forced out. Men, women and children – away they all go.

They have to sell all their things, which are worth very little. When they have spent the money from that, they have no more money. What can they do but steal and then be hanged, or go about begging?

From 'Utopia', by Sir Thomas More, 1516.

B

SOURCE

The treatment of beggars.

C

SOURCE

Paid to Henry Bradshaw when his wife gave birth:
– a shilling.
Paid for mending widow Chamley's shoes:
– ten pence.

From the Poor Law accounts for Glossop, Derbyshire, in the 1600s.

D

SOURCE

This print was made in 1577. It shows a beggar being whipped.

Beggars

Few people wrote about the poor. Poor Law accounts list the poor who were helped, as do parish records. They only have the bare facts. Here are some examples.

1548 *Robert Shakesbury*, a child, was whipped and sent out of London for pretending to have fits to make money by begging.

1580 *Elizabeth Whalley*, a pregnant woman, found sleeping in the street. Given 12 pence and ordered to go home to Norwich.

1598 *Joan Wood*, arrested for begging while visiting her son in prison in Leicester.

1635 *Ellen Dixon*, a blind woman, begging without a licence. Whipped and put in the stocks at Windermere.

1640 *William Clay*, a man with no legs, was begging without a licence. He was sent to prison and made to work at making gloves.

3.3 England and Britain

London and the south-east

London was where the English monarchs spent most of their time. Parliament was held in London, too. But the laws that were passed in London had to be obeyed by everyone. London was the centre of trade and industry. The way people in London spoke and wrote became 'standard English'.

The north-west

These areas were poorer than the area around London. It took longer for new ideas to get to these places, and longer for laws to be carried out. But different areas were famous for different things. There was Cornish tin, Yorkshire cloth and Devon sailors. It helped that Queen Elizabeth I was a popular monarch, and that the war against Spain united the whole country.

Wales

The Tudor monarchs came from Wales. This helped to keep Wales under control. The Welsh leaders learned English. Wales was ruled like England. There were Welsh MPs in Parliament in London.

Scotland

Scotland and England were old enemies but things changed. Both countries were Protestant. The new Bible for the Church of Scotland was written in 'standard English'. James, the King of Scotland, would also be the King of England when Elizabeth died.

A

SOURCE

This picture, from the 1600s, shows printers at work. Many men, but hardly any women could read by the early 1600s.

B

They rejected these designs:

They used this one:

SOURCE

Some Union Flags, designed in the early 1600s, for King James I of Great Britain.

SOURCE C

A modern photograph of Jesus College, Oxford, founded in 1571. Only men were allowed to go to university.

Elizabeth dies

In 1603 Elizabeth died. James became King James I of England and King James VI of Scotland.

James moved to London at once. Many Scottish people came with him. The two countries did not unite. But, in 1604, James took a new title – King of Great Britain.

SOURCE D

No one who speaks just Welsh can have a job helping to run Wales.

From a law passed in 1536.

SOURCE E

A modern photograph of Stratford-on-Avon Grammar School, set up in 1548. Shakespeare probably went to school here. The school only took boys.

Shakespeare

William Shakespeare (1564–1616) is the world's most famous playwright. He was born in Stratford-upon-Avon. He went to London in the late 1580s. He became an actor, poet and playwright. He wrote at least 36 plays. His plays were very popular at the time, and are still performed today.

Shakespeare lived in London but returned to Stratford from time to time. He died there in 1616.

Ireland

There was often trouble in Ireland. The English who lived there had married into Irish families. They spoke Irish as well as English. The English did not trust them.

Plantation

The English needed to find a way to pay for the English army in Ireland. They took land away from the Irish. The land was sold to English people. Parliament hoped that these settlers would help to keep Ireland under control. This system was called 'plantation'.

Religion

Ireland was a Catholic country. The new settlers were English Protestants. Churches in Ireland were made to use the English Bible and Prayer Book. The Catholics were not happy with this.

Rebellion

The Catholic Irish were helped by Philip II of Spain. He sent soldiers to help the Irish to fight the English. But Elizabeth sent a very large army to defeat the Irish rebellion. By 1603 the English had, for the first time, complete control of Ireland.

The Ulster plantation

The Irish who fought Elizabeth came mainly from Ulster. Under a government plan English and Scots people went to settle there. The Irish were to keep only the poor land. The plan did not work properly. Some Irish people were allowed to stay if they paid high rents for their land or worked for the settlers. So, many people still lived around the new settlers.

F **SOURCE** All English people, even in Dublin, speak Irish. The have Irish manners and clothes.

This was said by an Englishman who visited Ireland in 1578.

G **SOURCE** Sir Humphrey Gilbert ordered that the heads of those who were killed should be laid out so that nobody could come to his tent without passing through a lane of heads.

Written by a Englishman in 1575. He was describing the fighting between the English and the Irish at this time.

This print shows Elizabeth I's Lord Deputy in Ireland. It was printed in an English book in 1581.

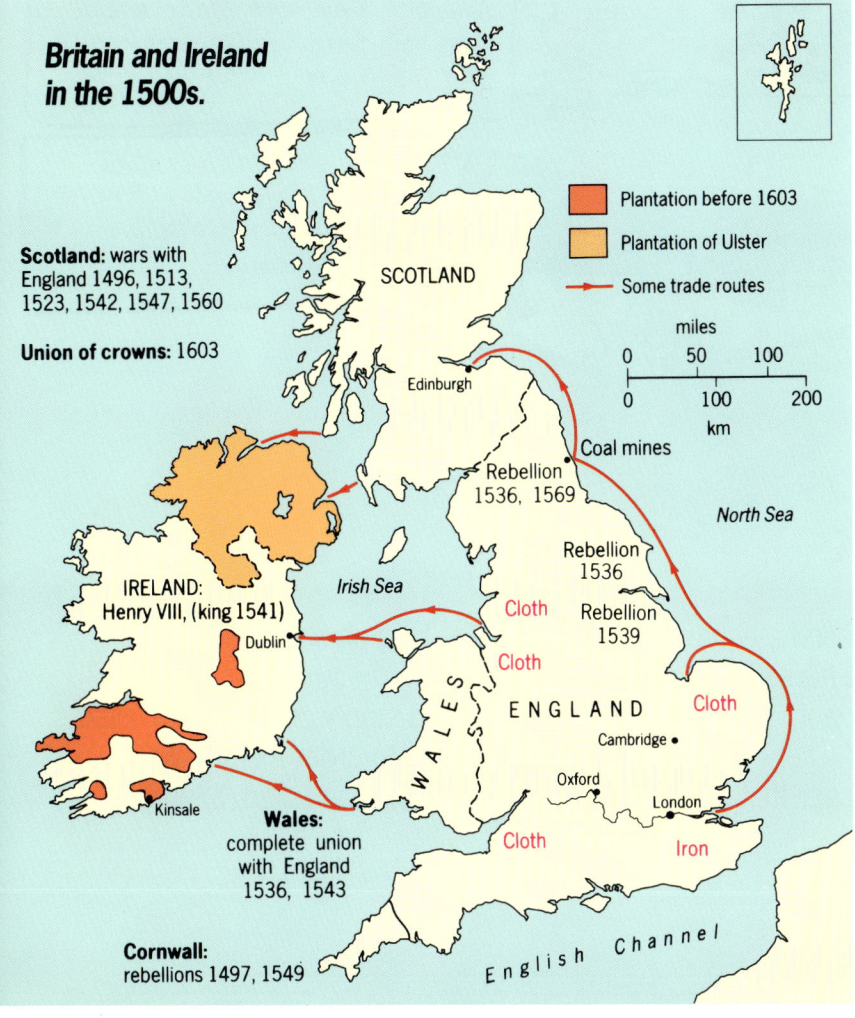

Britain and Ireland in the 1500s.

Scotland: wars with England 1496, 1513, 1523, 1542, 1547, 1560

Union of crowns: 1603

Plantation before 1603

Plantation of Ulster

Some trade routes

SCOTLAND

Edinburgh

miles
0   50   100

0   100   200
km

Coal mines

Rebellion
1536, 1569

North Sea

Rebellion
1536

Rebellion
1539

Irish Sea

Cloth

IRELAND:
Henry VIII, (king 1541)

Dublin

Cloth

W A L E S

E N G L A N D

Cloth

Cambridge ●

Oxford

London

Cloth

Iron

Kinsale

Wales:
complete union with England 1536, 1543

Cornwall:
rebellions 1497, 1549

English Channel

The Earl of Tyrone

Hugh O'Neill (about 1540–1616), the Earl of Tyrone was the son of an Irish noble who was brought up at the Court of Queen Elizabeth I. When he went back to Ireland he felt more English than Irish. He sided with the English when there were quarrels there.

Then O'Neill became the leader of his clan. He switched his loyalty to the Irish. The Irish were mostly Catholic. The English were mostly Protestant. To keep Ireland loyal to her, Elizabeth sent English Protestants to live in Ireland. They got the best land, houses and jobs. The Irish were bitter about this.

O'Neill led a rising against the English Protestants. But O'Neill was not a good leader. He argued with the other Irish leaders. So the English crushed the Irish rebellion. In 1607 O'Neill and several other Irish leaders fled to Rome.

3.4 People and Houses

Until about 1500, most houses in Britain were made of wood with thatched roofs. During the 1500s and 1600s new houses were made out of stone and brick. Many of these houses are still around today.

The queen keeps good peace in England now. This damp old castle is no use any more.

Every year we do better, husband! Tis time we pulled down our smokey house and built a better one, with one of those chimneys and walls of stone.

Glass windows in a house; it's like a church! What a good idea - they let the light in and keep the wind out.

No stone near here and oak costs far too much. But now we've got plenty of bricks.

The lands of Woburn Abbey would join nicely on to my estate. Now the king has made me Earl of Bedford, I need the sort of house fit for my title.

What magnificent style! When I get home I must copy these Italian buildings.

Bess of Hardwick

Bess (1518–1607) had four husbands, each richer than the last. Bess wanted herself and her children to be rich and important.

Bess was once told by an astrologer that she would not die as long as she was building something. In 1607 the winter was so bad the builders had to stop work. Bess travelled in the cold and wet to order them to work. She caught a bad cold and died, aged 89.

The royal palaces

Monarchs had lots of palaces. Palaces had great halls for meetings, feasts, dances, music and plays. They had kitchens, store-rooms, stables and places for servants to sleep. It was very important for the king or queen to show how rich, successful and up-to-date they were.

Hardwick Hall, Derbyshire, built by Elizabeth, the Countess of Shrewsbury, in 1597.

The gentleman's house

A country gentleman needed a large hall. He might hold the manor court there, or sit there as a JP to deal with criminals. But he needed comfortable private rooms too. If he hoped to be chosen as an MP, he had to entertain people.

A late 16th-century yeoman's house in Edwardstone, Suffolk.

Houses of the tenant farmers and the poor

We know less about these houses. Few, if any, still exist. A tenant farmer did not own his farm. He repaired the thatch or the walls, maybe built a fireplace and chimney at one end. We know the poor got poorer, so their houses probably became damper, draughtier and more unhealthy.

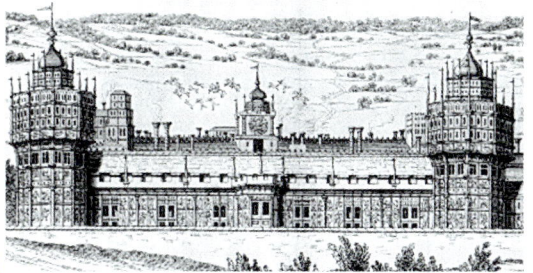

Nonsuch Palace, Surrey, built by Henry VIII.

The great houses of the nobles

Nobles had to impress people too. There had to be room for 50 or 60 people, family, servants and visitors. If the house was about 100 miles from London, the monarch might come to stay. This was such an honour that people built extra rooms, to give the right impression.

Little Moreton Hall, Cheshire.

The yeoman's house

A rich yeoman had no need to show off. But yeomen did want to be comfortable, and they could afford it. They had proper fireplaces, glass in the windows and plenty of food on the table.

4.1 The Gunpowder Plot

The Plot

In 1605, England had laws against people who were Catholics. A group of Catholics made a plan to change things. The plot was to blow up King James I when he opened Parliament on 5 November, and have a Catholic king instead.

The Letter

On 4 November, Lord Mounteagle, a Catholic, was given a letter. It told him not to go to Parliament the next day. He gave the letter to Robert Cecil. Cecil helped run the country for King James I.

A

SOURCE

Guy Fawkes

Guy Fawkes (1570–1606) was born in York. His family were Catholics. England was Protestant under the reign of Elizabeth I.

Fawkes went to live in Holland, where he became a soldier and fought the Protestant Dutch in Holland.

Fawkes became involved in a Catholic plot to kill King James 1 and replace him with a Catholic king. In 1605, the plotters hid gunpowder under the House of Lords. Fawkes was caught there, just about to light the fuse.

Fawkes was brave. He admitted he had been trying to kill the king. He would not name the other plotters. But he was tortured and eventually named them. The others were caught. They were all tried for treason. They were executed.

my lord out of the loue i beare ~~~~ To some of youer freud3 i haue acaer of youer preseruacion therfor i woulzl... aduyse yowe as yowe Tender youer lyf To deuys~some epscuse To shift of youer attendance at This parleament for god aud man hathe concurred To punishe The wickednes of this tyme and thinke not slightly e of this aduertisment but retiere youre self into youre coutri whyeare yowe~~ maye expect the event In saffti for Thowghe Theare be no apparance of anai stir yet i saye They shall receue a Terrible blowe This parleament and yet They shall not seie who hurts Them This counceL is not To be a contemned becaust it maye do yowe good and can do yowe no harme for The dangere is passed as soon as yowe haue burnt The letter and i hope god will giue yawe The grace To mak good use of it To whose holy proteccion icomend yowe

To the ryght honorable
The lord mounteagle

The letter sent to Lord Mounteagle.

Guy Fawkes

Soldiers searched Parliament. They found Guy Fawkes in a cellar, with barrels of gunpowder. He was tortured, and told the whole story. After a trial, the plotters were executed for treason. People were happy that the plot had failed.

The whole story?

Some people say that Robert Cecil knew about the plot all the time. He made it easy for the plotters because he wanted to catch them at the last minute. This would make people hate the Catholics even more.

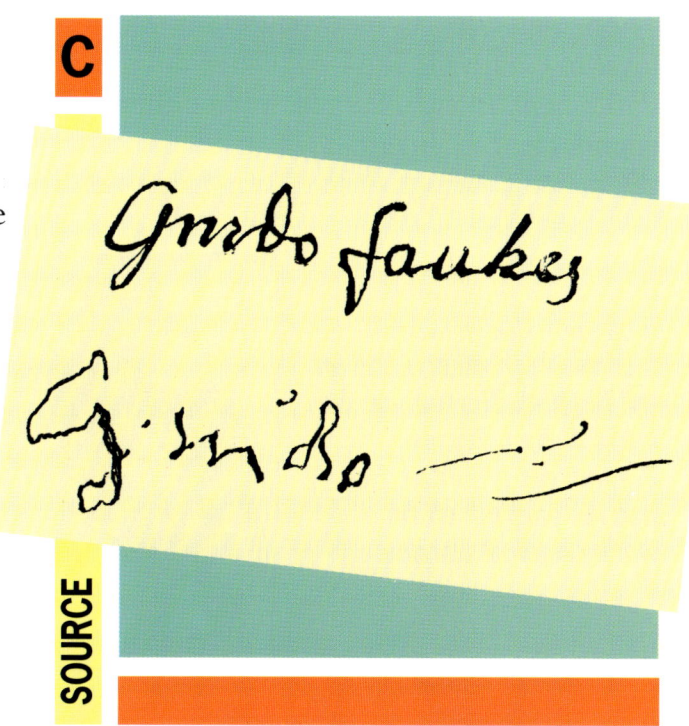

Fawkes' signature before and after torture.

4.2 1603–40: What Went Wrong?

Elizabeth I was a very popular queen. She got on well with Parliament. But by 1640, Parliament and the king were against each other. Why did this happen?

Buckingham

Elizabeth had favourites (nobles who she liked and gave presents and rewards to). But she was clever enough to keep other important people on her side too. James I and Charles I did not do this.

The Duke of Buckingham was a favourite of James I. The other nobles did not like him. He took the presents that James gave him and wanted presents for his friends and relatives too. He tried to make himself more popular by joining in wars on the Continent. But the attacks he led in Spain and France were flops. In 1628, Buckingham was murdered.

Laud and Strafford

Laud was Archbishop of Canterbury. The Earl of Strafford ruled the north of England and Ireland for King Charles I. These men were his most important mnisters. They were loyal to Charles I. Too loyal. They did not think about Parliament enough. People disliked them. They had lots of enemies in Parliament.

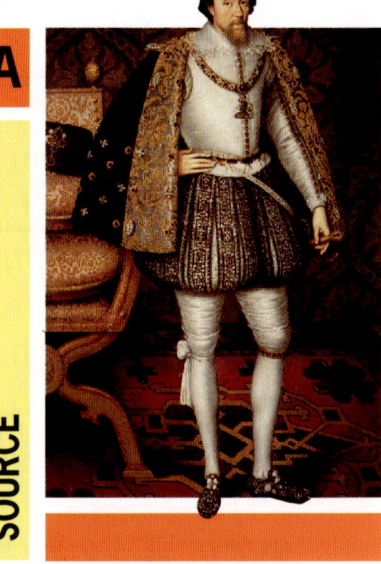

A **SOURCE**

A painting of King James I, painted during his lifetime.

A cartoon drawn in 1640. It shows Archbishop Laud (in the big hat). The man on the left is William Prynne. Prynne was a Puritan. He had his ears cut off for writing against bishops.

B **SOURCE**

A picture of the House of Commons, drawn in 1624. The Speaker is sitting in the big chair. The Speaker keeps control in the House of Commons.

The Church and the Puritans

The Puritans did not get on with the Church of England. They did not want bishops to run the Church. They believed God had chosen them to lead the fight against sin. King Charles I and Archbishop Laud believed, just as strongly, that God had chosen **them** to lead the Church. Puritans wrote books to spread their ideas. Laud banned Puritan books. Puritan writers, like Prynne (see Source B), were punished.

The King and money

Both James I and Charles I spent a lot of money. They often called Parliament to vote them extra money. When Parliament was called, the MPs wanted the king to listen to their complaints. The MPs said what they thought was wrong with the country and the Church. The king did not like this. In 1629, Charles I and Parliament quarrelled badly. Between 1629 and 1640, Parliament was not called.

Archbishop Laud

William Laud (1573–1645) was made Archbishop of Canterbury by Charles I. Laud was against the Puritans and tried to stop them printing books which explained their ideas. He wrote much of the new Prayer Book that was being forced on the Scots. Lots of people hated him.

Parliament accused him of treason in 1640. This was nonsense, for he had worked with the king. But he was found guilty and executed.

Raising money without Parliament

Charles I still needed to get money from somewhere. He did not want to call Parliament. How else could he get money? He found some old taxes which kings used to raise in Medieval times. They could raise these taxes without calling Parliament.

Ship money was a tax which was supposed to be collected only if there was a war, to pay for extra ships to fight the enemy. It was only supposed to be collected from places on the coast. Charles collected this tax from all over England. Ship money was legal, but the way Charles was using it seemed, to many people, to stretch the law.

The king and the law

The king chose judges, and sacked them if he didn't like them. He also ran special courts, like the Star Chamber. The Star Chamber had no jury, so the king could do what he wanted. He could fine people, put them in prison, or even cut their ears off. The special courts seemed to put the king above the law.

The Church of Scotland

Charles I wanted to change the Scottish Church. He wanted it to be more like the Church of England. In 1637, there were riots in Scottish churches when he said the English Bible and prayer book had to be used.

War with Scotland

In 1639, Charles sent soldiers to Scotland to make the Scots obey him. The English were beaten. Charles badly needed money to fight the Scots.

D

SOURCE

A picture of King Charles I, painted in 1633.

John Hampden

John Hampden was an MP. In 1636 he refused to pay his ship money. He said it was against the law.

After his trial, Hampden had to pay. But Parliament got rid of ship money in 1641.

E

SOURCE

It is against God to say that a king cannot do this or that.

Said by James I in 1616.

The Short Parliament

In 1640, Charles called Parliament. The MPs were very angry at not being called for so long. They did not want to vote taxes. They wanted to make King Charles agree to changes that Parliament wanted. Charles ended Parliament after just a few weeks.

The Scots in England

Charles raised an army with what little money he had. This army was beaten, and the Scots invaded England. Charles had to pay them £850 a day, or they would march on London. Only Parliament could give Charles that sort of money. What would Parliament want in return?

F **SOURCE**

A painting of Henrietta Maria in 1638. She was Charles I's wife. She was French and a Catholic.

G **SOURCE**

A cartoon about Scotland, in 1637. 'Arch Prelate' means Archbishop.

The Earl of Strafford

Thomas Wentworth (1593–1641) was the Earl of Strafford, and ruled the north of England and Ireland for Charles I in the 1630s. He thought that everyone should obey the king. Strafford was very hard on people who did not do what he said the king wanted them to do.

Charles I did not take Strafford's advice when he said the king should call Parliament in 1639. When Charles was forced to call Parliament, in 1640, there were many MPs who opposed him. Strafford suggested that Charles should arrest the most difficult MPs.

The MPs had Strafford arrested. They accused him of treason. Charles I promised to help him, but Strafford wanted to be tried. Strafford was executed for treason in 1641.

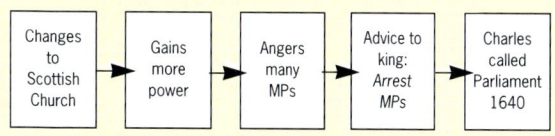

Changes to Scottish Church → Gains more power → Angers many MPs → Advice to king: *Arrest MPs* → Charles called Parliament 1640

Steps to Strafford's Fall

4.3 The Civil Wars

The Long Parliament

Parliament met again in November 1640. This Parliament is called the Long Parliament, because it sat until 1653. Parliament had Charles at its mercy. Charles needed money to pay the Scots army. He had to get the money from Parliament. The MPs saw they could force Charles to make changes. Laud and Strafford were arrested for treason. Parliament decided Strafford was guilty. Charles signed the death warrant. He had no choice. Parliament made more laws which took away other powers of the king. Charles agreed to them. Then the MPs agreed to taxes to pay the Scots.

Ireland

In October 1641 there was a rebellion in Ireland. The Catholic Irish murdered many Protestant settlers. An army had to go to deal with the problem. The king commanded the army. But Parliament did not trust the king with an army. They wanted someone else in charge.

The arrest of the five MPs

Some MPs now felt that Parliament was trying to take too much power from the king. Charles I began to have some support in the House of Commons. Then Charles made a mistake. He went to the House of Commons to arrest the five MPs that he thought were causing most trouble. Charles showed that he could not be trusted.

In 1641, King Charles agreed:

1 To call a parliament at least every three years.
2 Not to raise taxes unless Parliament agreed.
3 To give up his special law courts.

John Pym

John Pym (1584–1643) was born in Somerset. He became an MP. He led the House of Commons in their attacks on Charles I's policies. He knew a lot of people and he knew the right way to organize protests. He used pamphlets and news sheets to spread his views.

Pym was one of the MPs that Charles tried to arrest in 1642.

Pym organized the taxes to pay for the Civil War and arranged for the Scots to side with Parliament. He died in 1643. He was the one man who might have made the king keep to a settlement.

The First Civil War, 1642–46

Charles I was no longer willing to do what Parliament wanted. He and Parliament both started to raise armies.

1642–44: Many battles, no clear winner.

1643: The Scots agreed to help Parliament.

1644: Parliament and the Scots beat Charles I at Marston Moor.

1645: Parliament trained a new army – the New Model Army. This won a battle at Naseby.

By 1646: Charles I was a prisoner.

Problems in the army

People in the army wanted to vote in the elections for Parliament, like landowners did. They wanted to be able to worship God their way.

The Second Civil War, 1648

While he was in prison, Charles made a deal with the Scots. They agreed to help him to fight Parliament. A new civil war began. It did not last long. The Scots were beaten at Preston.

Why the New Model Army always won.

First rate training and discipline

Top quality weapons

Regular pay (except in 1647). The army cost about a million pounds a year

The Civil Wars, 1642–51.

- ■ Main sea ports
- ✕ Battles
- → Parliament's navy
- Royalist areas in 1642

0   50 miles
0   100 km

The trial of the king

Oliver Cromwell was an MP. He trained the New Model Army and led it to victory. Cromwell and many other MPs believed that they could never trust King Charles I. They believed that God had wanted Parliament to win, and that Charles had to go. Parliament set up a special court and Charles I was put on trial. Not all MPs agreed with this.

Execution of the king

It was clear that Charles I would be sentenced to death. He showed great courage and strength during the trial. On January 30, 1649, Charles I was executed.

No king

Laws were passed to make England a republic. This means that there was no monarch. For the next four years the MPs ruled England.

Charles Stuart

Charles I's son was Charles Stuart. He said he was now king. He tried to raise an army to take the country back. The MPs knew that Charles would get support in Scotland and Ireland.

Ireland and Scotland

Oliver Cromwell went to Ireland. He defeated Charles Stuart's supporters as well as the Irish Catholics. He went to Scotland and defeated the Scots. But Charles Stuart still marched into England. In 1651 Cromwell defeated Charles at Worcester. Charles managed to escape.

Some arguments about what to do with Charles I in 1648–49.

SOURCE

Sir Thomas Fairfax

Sir Thomas Fairfax (1612–71) organized a Yorkshire army to fight on the side of Parliament in the Civil War. Sir Thomas had trained as a soldier and had fought in Holland and France. He understood fighting, which not many people did.

When Parliament decided to set up the New Model Army they put Fairfax in charge. This was partly because he had experience of fighting, and also because he was not an MP. Both these things made the army obey him.

Fairfax believed that Parliament had been right to fight the king. When people began to talk of executing him, Fairfax did not speak up about it, either for execution or against it. He refused to be a judge at the trial. He retired to his lands in Yorkshire.

When the Protectorate collapsed, Fairfax advised the army leaders to restore the monarchy. In 1660 he was elected an MP and was sent to invite the new king, Charles II, back to England to rule.

4.4 Britain Without a King

Religion and government

The Civil Wars gave people the chance to say what they thought about the Church and the government. Here are some of the things which people talked about.

1 Should the country have just one religion?
2 Should people be allowed to worship in their own way?
3 Why had God let the king be beaten and executed?
4 How should the country be ruled now?
5 Should ordinary people vote in elections, as well as people who owned land?

Lots of books and pamphlets were written about these questions and ideas. Sources A, B, C and E show you some of them.

The army

The new ideas about religion and how to run the country were strong in the army. But the people in power thought ordinary people should be kept in their place. Even most of the Parliamentary generals, like Cromwell, believed that the rich and gentry should hold onto their power. Everyone agreed that Protestants should be able to worship God in their own way. But Catholics could not.

The Commonwealth, 1649–53

In 1649 England was a republic, a country with no king or queen. Parliament raised money to run the country by making new taxes. They also fined Royalists for fighting for the king. The army helped the MPs to keep control of the country. The navy stopped France and Spain helping the Royalists.

SOURCE A

The cover of 'The World Turned Upside Down', a pamphlet written in about 1647.

SOURCE B

God says 'Bishops, Charles and the Lords have had their turn. Whoever opposes me, your turn will be next.'

Written in 1650.

SOURCE C

We have shown how highly we value our freedom. To avoid being like slaves again, the people shall choose a Parliament every two years.

Written in 1647.

Ireland

Irish people were sent away from their land by Cromwell's men.

The war with the Dutch

Dutch ships carried goods from many countries in and out of Britain. In 1651 Parliament passed a law which said foreigners could only trade in their own goods. This caused a war in 1652–54. England won.

Cromwell gets rid of the Rump

The Rump were the MPs that were left from the Long Parliament. It was the Rump that ran the country. They did not make many improvements. They did not agree with the army. By 1653 the army was fed up. Cromwell and the army got rid of the MPs by force.

D SOURCE

I do not find anything in the law of God that says a Lord should choose twenty MPs, a gentleman two and a poor man none.

From a speech made in 1647.

E SOURCE

Parliament said: 'Risk your lives with us and we will make you free people.' So we claim the common lands bought by our money and blood.

Written in 1650.

F SOURCE

No man has the right to share in the affairs of the Kingdom if he owns no property.

From a speech made in 1647.

John Lilburne

John Lilburne (about 1614–57) fought on the side of Parliament during the Civil War. When the New Model Army was formed he refused to join it, so did not fight after 1645.

Lilburne felt that people had a right to say what they thought and to write books and pamphlets about whatever they wanted. He thought that every man should be able to vote for MPs. These were all seen as dangerous ideas at the time. Every government from 1637 to 1654 either put him in prison or exiled him for writing about his ideas.

People, especially the ordinary people in the towns, agreed with his ideas. He formed a group of people who thought the same way as he did. They were called the Levellers.

The Protectorate, 1653–59

The army leaders tried to find a way of ruling England that would make it a better place. They asked Cromwell to become king, and work with Parliament. Cromwell said no. He did not believe in monarchy. Cromwell was made ruler for life. He was called the Lord Protector.

Cromwell

Many people trusted and admired Cromwell. He was an ordinary gentleman who had become ruler of a country. People thought that this was God's work. Cromwell tried hard to work with Parliament. But he could not keep both Parliament and the army happy.

War with Spain

England now had a powerful army and navy. In 1655 Cromwell sent the navy to attack the Spanish West Indies. Jamaica was taken. The navy also stopped ships loaded with American silver from getting back to Spain. Then Cromwell sent the army to help the French fight the Spanish. In 1659 the Spanish were defeated.

The death of Cromwell

Cromwell died in 1658. His son, Richard, became Lord Protector. In 1659, Richard Cromwell gave up the job. Now the army had no leader. The wars had cost a lot of money. There was no money to pay the army. What would happen next?

G SOURCE

A painting of Oliver Cromwell, in about 1650.

H SOURCE

A cartoon printed in 1653. A law banned Christmas parties. Father Christmas is in the middle.

I SOURCE

His Highness the Lord Protector of the Commonwealth of England, Scotland and Ireland.

Part of Cromwell's title as Lord Protector.

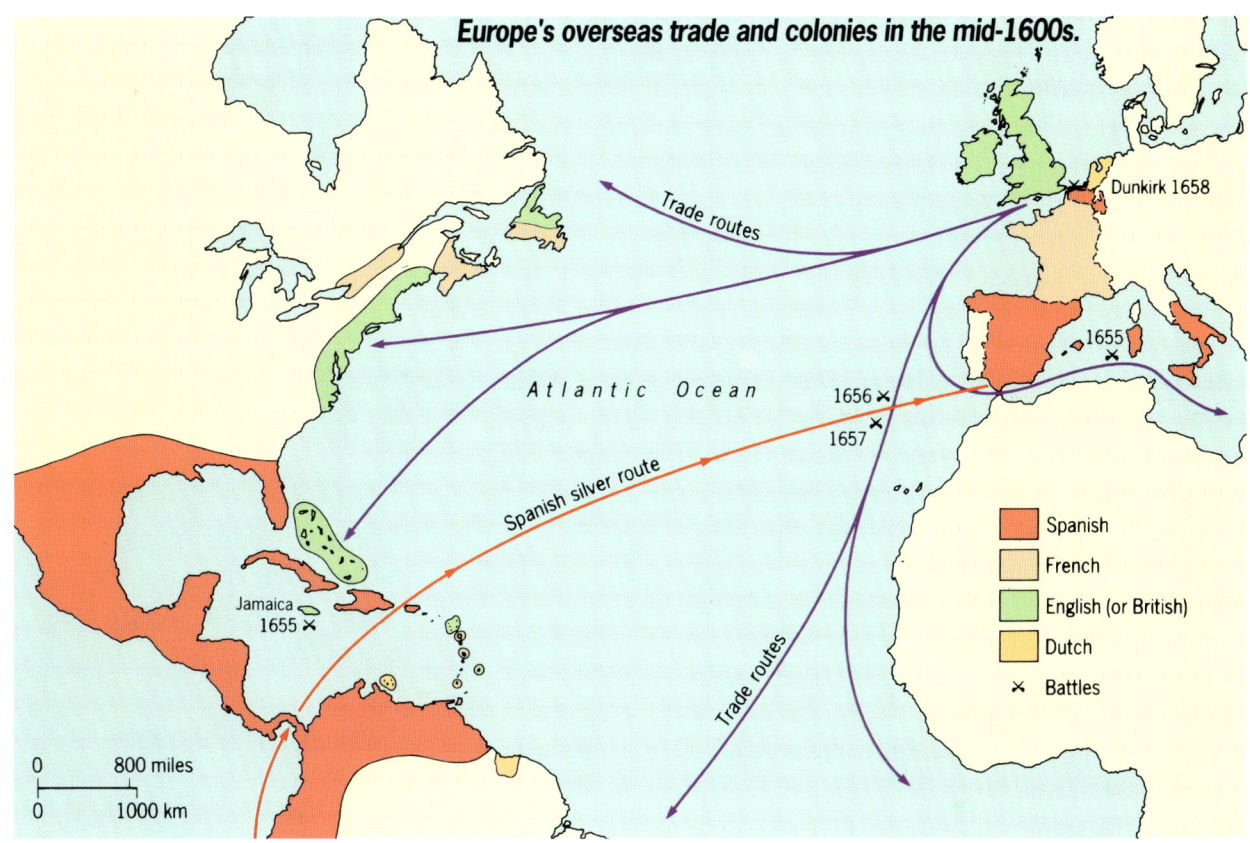

Europe's overseas trade and colonies in the mid-1600s.

Trade routes

Atlantic Ocean

Dunkirk 1658

1655

1656 ×

1657 ×

Spanish silver route

Jamaica
1655 ×

Trade routes

	Spanish
	French
	English (or British)
	Dutch
×	Battles

0   800 miles
0   1000 km

Oliver Cromwell

Oliver Cromwell (1599–?) was born in Cambridgeshire. Cromwell was a Puritan. He was MP for Cambridgeshire. When the Civil War broke out he organized his own cavalry regiment to fight in the Civil War. In 1645 he helped to organize the New Model Army.

The New Model Army were well trained and well equipped. They were paid fairly regularly too. This was unlike the other troops on both sides. Cromwell was an excellent army leader and battle planner. His army never lost a battle. The New Model Army were the reason why Parliament won the Civil War.

Cromwell believed the country should be run by an elected Parliament. He wanted Charles I to agree to rule with less power. But when he saw that Charles would not agree he said that Charles should be executed. As leader of the Army, Cromwell had a lot of power. He was also accepted by a lot of MPs. He tried to organize the running of the country by Parliament. But the parliaments failed to run the country properly. Cromwell took over running the country. He was offered the crown but refused it. He ran the country as Lord Protector, governed by rules very like those he had asked Charles to accept.

4.5 Monarchy Restored

Back to normal

In 1660, Parliament asked Charles II to come back as king. King Charles II was to rule with Parliament with the limits on his power set in 1641 (see page 38). Parliament also brought back the Church of England.

A problem for the future

Charles was secretly a Catholic. James, his brother, was openly a Catholic. Charles had no children by his wife. So James would be king when Charles died. How would Protestant Britain take to a Catholic king?

Plague and fire

The plague killed over 100,000 people in London in 1665. It killed a lot of people in the countryside as well. It was spread by fleas which were carried around by rats.

London had always had a lot of fires. Most houses were built of wood and thatch. But the Great Fire of 1666 was very bad. It burned down most of the centre of London. A man called Samuel Pepys lived in London during the plague and Great Fire. He kept a diary. It tells us how the plague and the fire spread through the city. It also tells us how people felt as it was happening. There was a lot of rebuilding after the Great Fire. The new houses were built of brick, not wood. Soon London was bigger than ever.

B
SOURCE

Charles II, 1684. People believed that kings could cure people of scrofula (King's Evil) by touching.

Laws against Puritans

1 Only Church of England services allowed.
2 Puritans were not allowed to be teachers or priests.

The Great Fire of London, painted soon after it broke out in 1666.

A

SOURCE

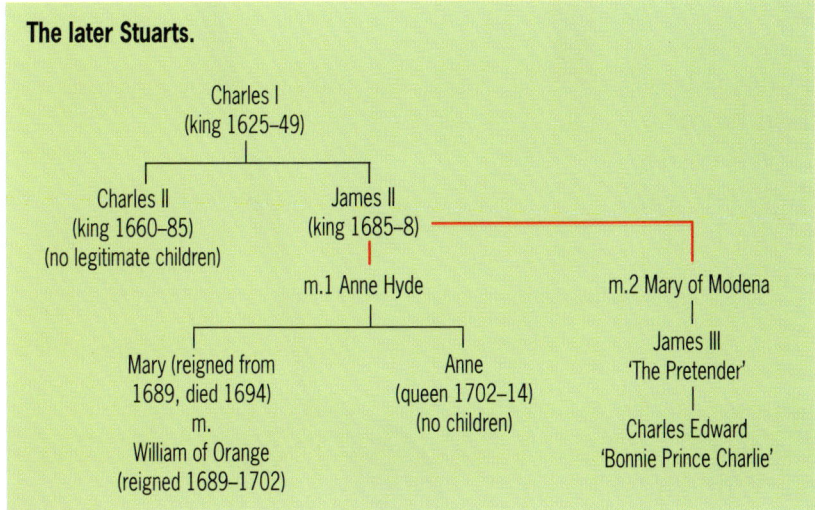

The later Stuarts.

Charles I
(king 1625–49)

Charles II
(king 1660–85)
(no legitimate children)

James II
(king 1685–8)

m.1 Anne Hyde

m.2 Mary of Modena

Mary (reigned from
1689, died 1694)
m.
William of Orange
(reigned 1689–1702)

Anne
(queen 1702–14)
(no children)

James III
'The Pretender'

Charles Edward
'Bonnie Prince Charlie'

C

SOURCE

The fire began in Pudding Lane. In an hour the fire ranged every way – the wind was driving it into the city. After a long, dry spell everything burned very easily.

From Samuel Pepys's Diary, 2 September 1666.

D

People think that the fire was caused by some kind of plot. Many people have been arrested.

From Samuel Pepys's Diary, 6 September 1666.

E

People are generally happy that the fire was an accident.

From a letter by Sir T. Osborne, an MP, 2 October 1666.

F

The Frenchman, who is said to have started the fire and was hanged for it, confessed.

From Samuel Pepys's Diary, 24 February 1667. The Frenchman said he was a Catholic. He was hanged on 27 October 1666.

Samuel Pepys

Samuel Pepys (1633–1703) was a tailor. Pepys had a good education and in 1655 took a job as secretary to a rich cousin.

His cousin became an admiral and Pepys worked in the Navy Office in London from 1659 to 1689. From 1660 to 1669 Pepys kept a diary. It was a private diary. He wrote in code, so that only he could read it. It gives lots of details about the people he met and the things that he did and about his many girlfriends.

Pepys's Diary also talks about Charles II and James II, for he went to Court quite often. He also lived in London through the plague of 1665 and the Great Fire of 1666. His accounts of both events brings them to life.

The code in his diary was not cracked until 1825.

James II

When Charles II died in 1685, James II took over with little trouble. A rebellion by his nephew, the Duke of Monmouth, was easily put down. Nobody wanted another civil war. Besides, they thought they would not have to put up with a Catholic king for long.

Mary and William

James II had two Protestant daughters. The eldest, Mary, would become queen when James died. Mary's husband, William of Orange, was the Protestant leader of the Netherlands.

Changes

James II let Catholics become officers in the army. This was against the law. Parliament refused to change the law. So James ended Parliament and ignored the law. This was good for Catholics. Some of the laws he made without Parliament were good for other groups too. He said everybody could worship God in their own way. This was good for Protestants. But they still didn't support him.

A baby prince

James had a young second wife. In 1688, she and James had a son. Now there would be a Catholic king after James – not a Protestant queen!

A playing card, made in 1689, showing how the baby might have been smuggled in. 'Brought to bed' means 'had a baby'.

G SOURCE

Protestants said that the new prince was really a baby hidden in a warming pan like this and taken into the queen's room.

H SOURCE

II ♦

The Queen is brought to bed of a Boy

Reported so

Revolution, 1688

Parliament acted quickly. They asked William and Mary to bring an army to England to take over from James. When William landed in England many of James's soldiers and friends sided with William. James escaped to France.

A new Parliament

In 1689, a new Parliament said William and Mary were the new monarchs. They passed laws to stop a monarch ruling without Parliament. Parliament was now the most powerful part of this partnership.

Religion

Catholics and Protestants who were not in the Church of England could have their own services. But they could not become MPs, work in government or go to university.

New laws and other changes, 1688–1701

Kings and queens must:
1 Be Protestant.
2 Marry Protestants.
3 Call a new Parliament every three years.

Kings and queens cannot:
1 Have an army without Parliament agreeing.
2 Change laws.
3 Sack judges they don't like.

Paying the bills:
Parliament set taxes and controlled most government spending.

Margaret Fell

Margaret Fell (1614–1702) was married to Thomas Fell, a lawyer. Thomas was often away on business, so Margaret ran the household.

In 1652 George Fox, who had started the Quaker movement, persuaded Margaret to join the Quakers, also called The Society of Friends. They would not go to Church of England services, or pay Church taxes.

Thomas did not become a Quaker. But he did not mind Margaret joining. Their house became a centre for Quakers all over the north. When Thomas died in 1659, Margaret spent more time working for the Quakers. She married George Fox in 1669. They were often put in prison for their beliefs.

Margaret and George collected money to help Quakers in trouble. They set up groups all over England and even in the American colonies. Margaret and George both lived long enough to get religious freedom in 1689.

4.6 Britain takes a Lead in Science

Questioning

For a long time science was based on the ideas of the Ancient Greeks. Anything that did not fit in with their ideas was said to be wrong. Then, in the 1500s, people began to question these ideas. Science came to be based on what could be seen (observation) and tested (by experiment).

Copernicus

The Ancient Greeks said that the sun went around the earth. But Copernicus said that the earth went around the sun. Later scientists proved that Copernicus was right.

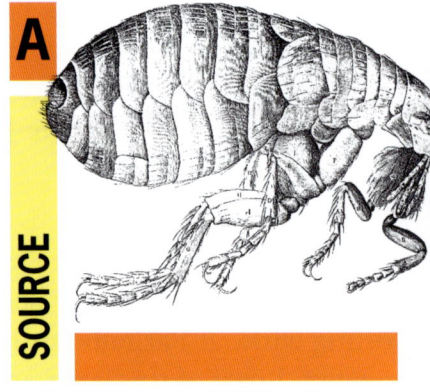

A flea drawn in 1665 using an early microscope.

William Harvey

In 1628, Harvey showed that blood circulated (went round and round) in the body. The Greeks had said that blood moved very differently. Harvey's idea did not help to cure people until much later. But he is important because he used experiments to prove his ideas. People could see that he was right. So they took up the idea of experimenting.

Before Copernicus

The Sun goes round the Earth in a circle every day. So do the planets and the Moon.

I agree, because it fits in with what the Bible says in Joshua, Chapter 10, verse 13.

Yes. The circle is a perfect shape - so the Sun is **bound** to move in a circle.

Me too. It fits in with all the famous Greek writers.

After Newton

The Earth goes around the Sun once a year. Its orbit is _not_ a circle.

It's the force of gravity that pulls the Earth and the Sun together.

Yes - It's the same force that pulls this apple down off the tree. Isaac Newton has measured it exactly.

Every time I check the measurements I get the same as Newton! His calculations are dead right too. You can't disagree.

The Royal Society

Science became fashionable in the 1660s. Charles II and others set up the Royal Society. The Royal Society did experiments and published books. Members of the Society talked about science and questioned the old ways of thinking. The Society helped develop physics, chemistry and other sciences. The Society also did other experiments, which seem less sensible now, like trying to turn metal into gold. But it was all part of the new thinking.

Sir Isaac Newton

Newton was a member of the Society. He put together the work of Copernicus and others. Newton showed how gravity held the sun and planets together. He was also able to work out the movement of the planets. Newton's work is still used in space science today.

B **SOURCE**

Greenwich Royal Observatory, built in 1676. It was used to look at the stars. By measuring stars from Greenwich, sailors, anywhere in the world, could work out where they were.

Isaac Newton

Isaac Newton (1642–?) was born in Lincolnshire. He left school when he was 14, to help his uncle run the family farm. But he was always reading, calculating and working out how things worked. His uncle sent him to Cambridge University in 1661.

In 1664, the plague hit Cambridge. Newton went back to the family farm until the plague was over. This was where he thought out most of his ideas. By 1669 Newton was a professor.

Isaac did not study one thing. He worked at maths. He wrote books on religion. He found out how a rainbow showed its colours, by working with light and prisms. He also worked out the theory of gravity.

Newton became a fellow of the Royal Society, a scientific group set up in 1660. He was later elected President of the Society. He was also MP for Cambridge for a time. Charles II knighted him and made him Master of the Royal Mint and he organized a new coinage.

5.1 Ireland and Scotland

Many people in Ireland and Scotland were unhappy that James II was no longer king.

Ireland

James II was a Catholic. He made things better for Irish Catholics. So, most people in Ireland wanted him back as king. In 1689 James II went to Ireland with a French army. He called a Parliament in Dublin. Laws were passed taking back land from the English and Scots settlers.

Ulster

But Ulster, in the north of Ireland, was not under James II's control. The people in charge were Protestant. The Protestants of Londonderry (see map) shut the gates of the city. They would not allow James II's army in. James cut off food to the city.

Battle of the Boyne

William and Mary sent ships with food to Londonderry. In 1690 William came to Ireland with an army. There was a battle between the armies of James and William. William won the Battle of the Boyne. This battle is remembered every July in Northern Ireland.

George Walker

George Walker (1618–90) was born in Ulster. He became a clergyman and settled to preach near Derry. In 1688 he raised a regiment of Protestant soldiers to fight James II.

In 1689 James advanced on Derry. Walker persuaded the Governor of Derry to leave the city and took it over. James besieged Derry. Walker led attacks on the besiegers. He organized the food, and even cooked rats. After 100 days the city was relieved. Walker died at the Battle of the Boyne.

A A 1980s wall painting in Londonderry. William is on the white horse on the left.

SOURCE

Return to France

James II lost his hold on Ireland. He went back to France. The Protestants were back in control of Ireland.

Laws against Catholics

The Protestant settlers brought in more laws against Irish Catholics. The laws would help to get rid of any Irish people who might lead a rebellion. Some Catholics went to France. Other Catholics became very poor. Some Catholics became Protestants. The Protestants ended up owning nearly all the land.

Scotland

Scotland is divided into two parts: the Highlands and the Lowlands. People in the Lowlands were mostly Protestant. People in the Highlands were mostly Catholic. Many of the Highlanders wanted James as king. They tried to rebel against William. William sent an army to Scotland. The army beat the Highlanders.

Jacobites

Many Scots people still believed that William should not be king. Many Highlanders still wanted James II back. These people were called Jacobites. 'Jacobite' comes from the Latin word for James.

Laws against Irish Catholics

A Catholic could not:

1 vote or be an MP.

2 go to university.

3 be a teacher.

4 be a soldier.

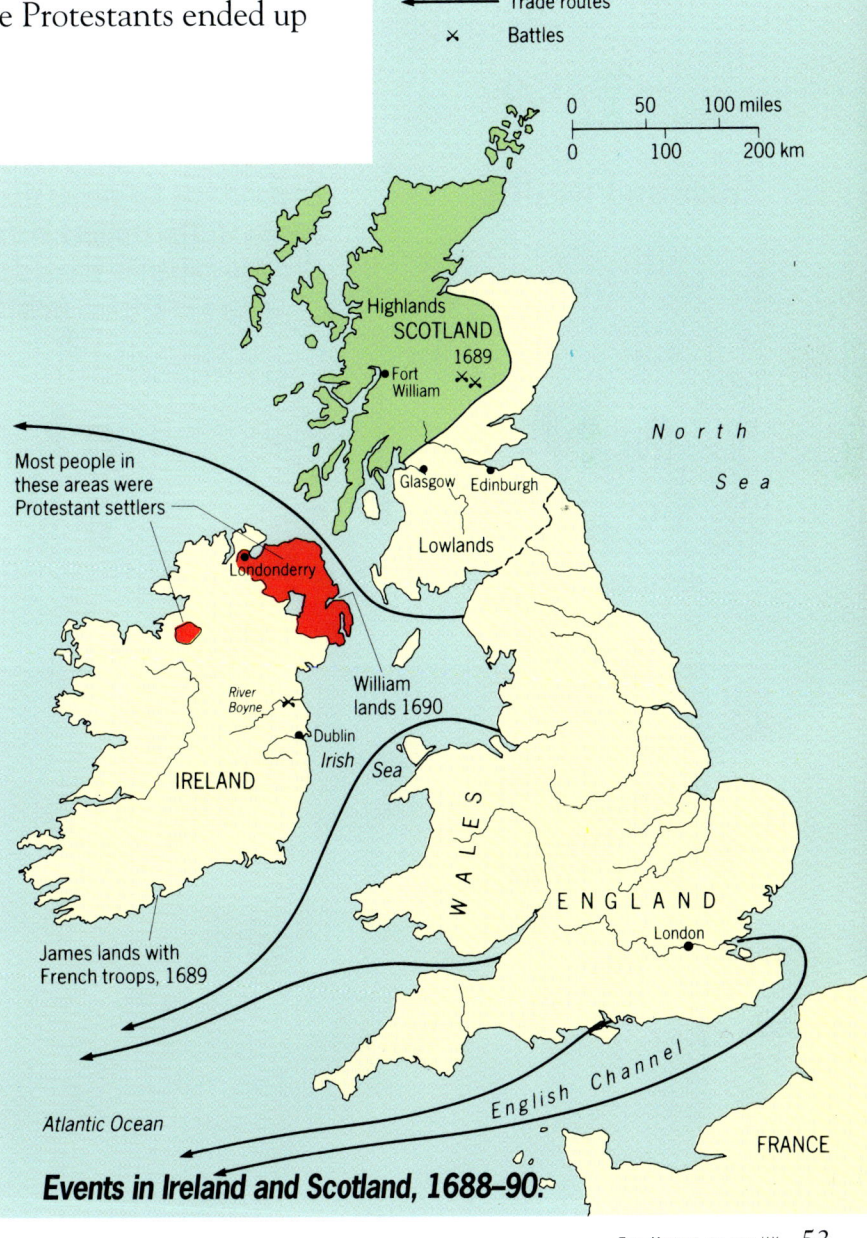

Events in Ireland and Scotland, 1688–90.

5.2 A Partly United Kingdom

In 1707 Scotland united with England. Scottish MPs now went to the Parliament in London. Why did this happen?

The Highlanders

Most members of Scotland's Parliament came from the lowlands. The lowlanders hated the highlanders more than they hated the English.

Trade and wealth

England was far richer than Scotland. The traders in the Scottish lowlands wanted to share in English wealth.

ENGLAND   SCOTLAND

SOURCE

The Battle of Culloden, painted in 1746.

Flora Macdonald

Flora Macdonald (1722–90) was brought up by rich relatives on the Isle of Skye.

In 1745 Prince Charles Stuart, on the run after the Battle of Culloden, fled to an island where Flora was staying. She met him and agreed to help him escape. She dressed him as a female servant and took him by rowing boat to Skye. Here her relatives (all Jacobites) helped him to escape to France.

The story got out and Flora was arrested. She was put in prison in London, but was later pardoned. Flora went to live in America, but returned to Scotland, where she died in 1790.

The Jacobites

When William and Mary died Mary's sister, Anne, became queen. It looked like Queen Anne would not have any children. Parliament wanted a German Protestant cousin of Anne's to become the next monarch. The danger was that Scotland might choose James II's Catholic son. The Jacobites saw him as the next king, James III. This could cause problems. That was a good reason to unite the two countries before Anne died.

Jacobite rebellions

Anne died in 1714. George of Hanover became king. In 1715 James II's son tried to claim the throne. There was a rebellion in Scotland. It was defeated.

The '45

This rebellion, in 1745, was led by James II's grandson. He became known as Bonnie Prince Charlie. He won control of a lot of Scotland, then marched into England. He got as far as Derby. The English did not join Bonnie Prince Charlie's army. He had to march back to Scotland.

Battle of Culloden

This was the final battle between the English army and the supporters of Bonnie Prince Charlie. The Jacobites were destroyed. Prince Charles escaped to France. Culloden was the last battle fought in Britain.

Results

There were no more Jacobite Rebellions. Lots of forts and roads were built in the Highlands. Highlanders had to give up their weapons and tartan kilts. Schools were set up where only English was used.

B

SOURCE

A cartoon, 'The Highland Visitors', published in London 1745.

The Act of Union, 1707

The Scots agreed to:

1 A single Parliament, in London.

2 Have Anne's German cousin as the next monarch.

The English agreed to:

1 Let the Scots trade on the same terms as the English.

2 Let the Scots contol their own Church and law courts.

5.3 Why did Britain Gain an Empire?

In 1603 Britain didn't own any land in other parts of the world. By 1750 Britain had lots of land in other parts of the world. These lands were called colonies. All of the colonies together was called an empire. People from Britain went to live in different parts of the Empire.

In some places in the Empire they farmed the land to feed themselves. In other places they grew crops that were expensive in Britain (like coffee and sugar) and used them to trade with Britain. A lot of the work was done by slaves (a slave is a person who is owned like a piece of property). The British Empire became the richest and most powerful empire in the world. Why did this happen?

Trading companies

It cost a lot of money to start a new colony. The money was needed for things like ships, tools, food and clothing. So London traders got together to share the costs of starting a new colony. These groups were called trading companies. The trading companies then made a lot of money by selling the tea, sugar, coffee and tobacco that were grown in the colonies.

Who went to the colonies?

1 People wanting adventure.
2 People wanting to be free to follow their own religion. (Many Puritans went to North America.)
3 People wanting land of their own.

The trading companies paid for people to travel to the colonies. But they had to agree to be an unpaid servant of the company for seven years. Often they were treated just like slaves, and bought and sold.

A SOURCE

The coat of arms and crest of John Hawkins. Hawkins made lots of money as a slave trader.

B SOURCE

They had no friends to welcome them. It was winter. They could see that it was a wilderness full of wild beasts and wild men.

Written by William Bradford in around 1645. He is remembering life in 1620.

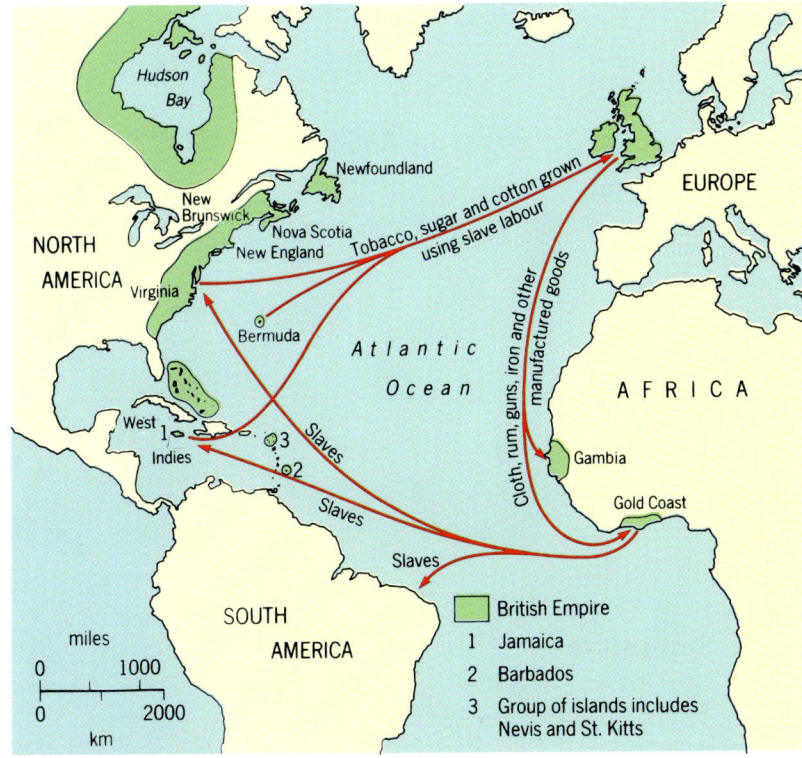

The 'triangular trade': how the traders turned slaves into sugar.

Some colonies gained by government action:

1655 Jamaica captured.

1660 Bombay given to Charles II as a wedding present.

1664 New York captured.

1704 Gibraltar captured.

1688–1713 Newfoundland, Nova Scotia and Hudson's Bay captured.

Slavery

People who grew sugar and tobacco said slaves were better than white workers. Slaves got no pay. They also said that black people worked better than white people in the heat.

Government action

The government saw that trade was important. They used the navy to protect the trade and keep foreigners out.

C SOURCE	Owned by James Stone	Value
	Thomas Groves, 4 years to serve	1,300 lbs of tobacco
	Emaniel, a negro man	2,000 lbs of tobacco
	Mingo, a negro man	2,000 lbs of tobacco

From a list of the property of James Stone, 1648.

Pocohantas

Pocohantas (1595–1617) was the daughter of an American Indian king in Virginia. There was an English settlement nearby and one of the settlers, John Smith, was captured by the Indians. Smith later said that she saved his life, but there is no evidence that her father would have killed him.

Pocohantas was friendly with the settlers. In 1613 she became a Christian and married Rolfe, a settler, in the same year. She called herself Rebecca. In 1616 the family came back to live in England. In 1617, just as they were getting ready to go back to America, she became ill. She died before they could return.

5.4 Britain's Growing Wealth

Trade

In 1750 British merchants could trade with 14 million people in the British Empire. Britain also led the rest of the world in trade. Britain had more ships than any other country. London was the largest city in Europe.

Industry

New industries, like sugar refining, grew. Some old industries, like the woollen cloth industry, grew too. Coal mining was also important. Lots of coal was sent to the rest of Europe.

Farming

In 1750, most people in Britain still lived by farming. New ways of farming were being used to grow more food. New crops like turnips could be used to feed cattle. This meant that there were more cattle. All this meant that food was cheap.

Transport

Roads were just mud tracks. Industries were set up near rivers or the sea. This meant that goods could be carried by boat. The best farming areas were near water too.

Trade and industry in the British Isles, 1650–1750.

Liverpool
Goods from the colonies, including cotton. Liverpool was also in the slave trade

Northern Ireland
New linen industry

Shropshire
New iron-working area. 1710: Abraham Darby invented a way to use coal instead of wood in the furnace to make cast iron

Dublin •

Bristol
Brings in and refines sugar and tobacco from the colonies

Cornwall
1711: the first successful steam engine made by Thomas Newcomen to pump water out of the mines

London

The city of London was like a spider at the centre of a web of British trade. Banks made it easy to borrow money and to pay money. People could buy and sell shares in the trading companies. Insurance companies would pay out money if a trader's ship was lost.

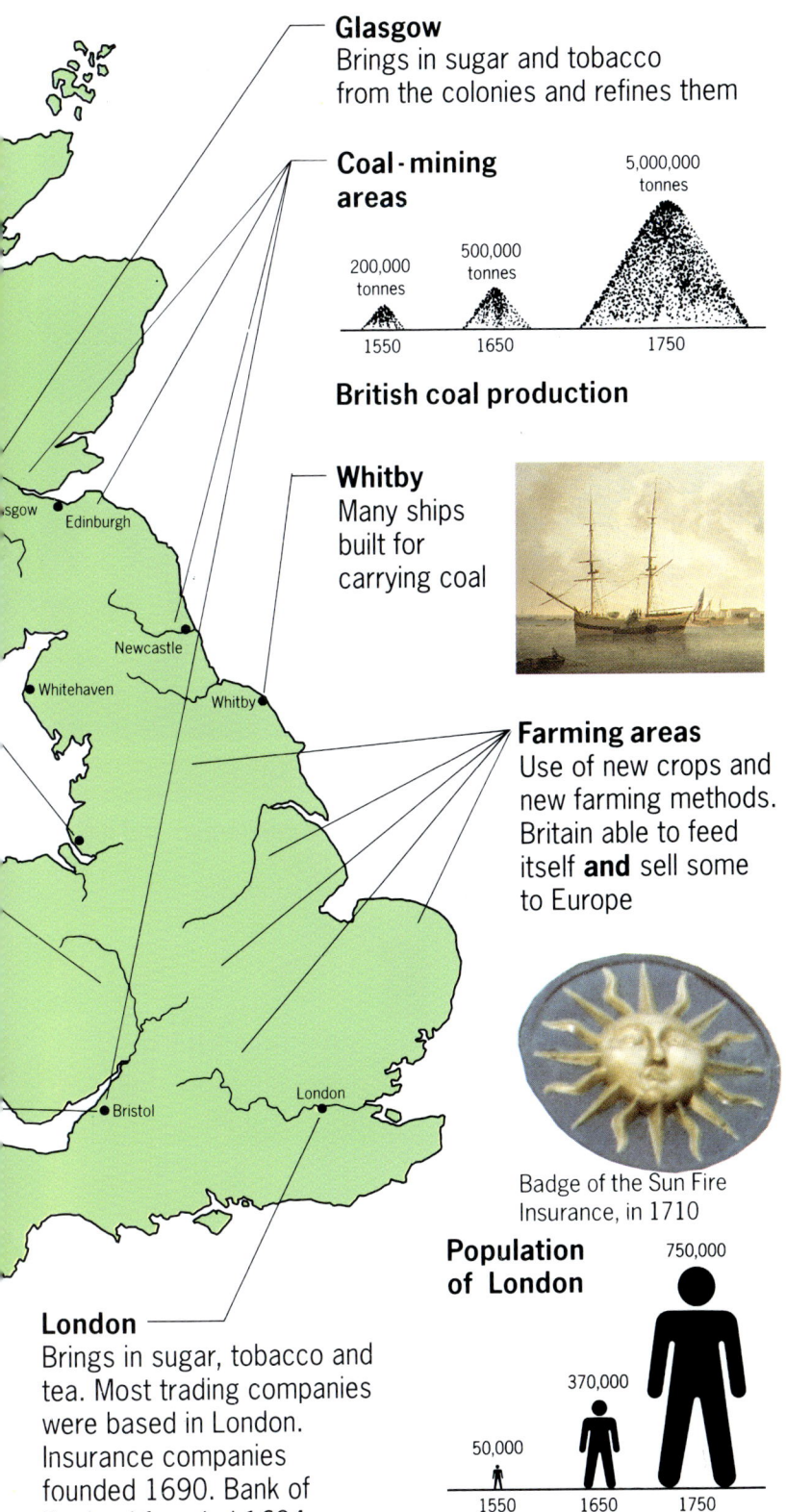

Glasgow
Brings in sugar and tobacco from the colonies and refines them

Coal-mining areas

5,000,000 tonnes

500,000 tonnes

200,000 tonnes

1550   1650   1750

British coal production

Whitby
Many ships built for carrying coal

Farming areas
Use of new crops and new farming methods. Britain able to feed itself **and** sell some to Europe

Badge of the Sun Fire Insurance, in 1710

Population of London

750,000

370,000

50,000

1550   1650   1750

sgow • Edinburgh
• Newcastle
• Whitehaven   • Whitby
• Bristol   • London

London
Brings in sugar, tobacco and tea. Most trading companies were based in London. Insurance companies founded 1690. Bank of England founded 1694.

Edward LLoyd

Edward Lloyd ran a coffee house in London in the 1680s. It became the best place to trade, to find out about what had happened to ships. The merchants who met there formed into a company which they called 'LLoyds of London'.

It still runs insurance and gives shipping information. Lloyd died in about 1726.

5.5 Rich and Poor in 18th-Century Britain

A country gentleman and his family, 1750.

The rich

Rich people all followed the same fashions in clothes, houses and way of life.

Country houses

These houses were big enough to hold many visitors and their servants. There were rooms for parties and dances. Young men finished their education by travelling around Europe. They brought back statues and paintings. These were put on show in the country houses.

London and Bath

Part of the year was spent in London. Part of the year was spent in a place like Bath. People showed off their expensive clothes and looked for the right person to marry. People married to get more money and land.

I came to villages of sad little huts made up of only stones piled together. I took them at first sight for a sort of barns to feed cattle in.

A description of the houses of the poor in Westmorland. Written by Celia Fiennes, who travelled round Britain in 1679.

A public execution in London, drawn by William Hogarth.

The poor

Prices fell, so wages could buy more. People were poorer in places like Ireland and Scotland. But there were some very poor people in England too. They suffered most if the harvest was not very good. They were supposed to have help from the money raised by the Poor Law if they stayed in their own villages.

Poor people in the towns lived in slums. They were crowded together, with no clean water to cook with or drink. People often died very young.

A woman showed us the cave where she lived. It was clean and neat. There was a whole side of bacon hanging up by the chimney.

Her husband worked in the lead mines. He could earn about five pence a day. If she worked hard washing the lead she could get three pence a day. That was eightpence a day to keep a man, his wife and five children. Yet they seemed to live very pleasantly – the children looked plump and fat.

From Daniel Defoe, 'Tour through the Whole Island of Great Britain', 1726. The cave was in Derbyshire.

William Hogarth

William Hogarth (1697–1764) taught himself to draw. He trained as an engraver, working on tankards and moved on to illustrating books. He was 30 years old before he learned to paint.

Hogarth decided to do a series of paintings that told a story. These would be separate paintings, but would tell the story in the way a comic strip does today. He made engravings of these pictures so that he could print lots of copies. The pictures were a great success.

5.6 The First 'Prime Minister'

The Cabinet

A group of ministers helped George I and George II run the country. This group was called the Cabinet. The cabinet was the name of the private room of the monarch, where the early meetings were held. One of the ministers was chosen to run the meetings. He had to get the king to agree to any decisions. He also had to get the MPs to agree, because they controlled the money.

Prime Minister

Sir Robert Walpole was very good at this job. He was the first one to be called Prime Minister ('prime' means 'first'). The name was later used for the head of the government.

Whitehall

Most of the government offices were in Whitehall. This is where the Cabinet met. It was close to the king's old palace of Whitehall. It was also close to the Houses of Parliament.

Number 10 Downing Street is just off Whitehall. This has been the Prime Minister's offical home ever since Walpole had it rebuilt to live in.

A SOURCE

A picture of Sir Robert Walpole, drawn at the time.

B SOURCE

No. 10 Downing Street, rebuilt for Walpole in 1736.

Sir George Downing

Sir George Downing (1623–84) was born in the American colonies. He came to England to join Cromwell's army in the Civil Wars. He worked as an ambassador for Cromwell, but changed sides in 1660. He helped Charles II to regain the throne. Charles gave him land and power as a reward, including land in London (where Downing Street is today).

6.1 The British Isles, 1500–1750

The British Isles in 1750.

- People speak English
- People speak Welsh
- People speak Gaelic
- • Towns with over 20,000 people

SCOTLAND

Glasgow
Edinburgh

Peaceful border

North Sea

IRELAND
All controlled by the British
Dublin

Liverpool • Manchester

WALES

Norwich •

• Birmingham

ENGLAND

• Bristol   London •
(750,000 people)

George II, King of Great Britain Ireland and the British colonies overseas

0   50   100 miles
0   100   200 km

English Channel

Channel Islands

FRANCE

The British Isles in 1500 (see page 4).

James IV, King of Scotland

SCOTLAND

Edinburgh

English–Scots border: many battles and raids

North Sea

IRELAND

The Pale – fully controlled by the English
Dublin

• York

WALES

Norwich •

ENGLAND

Oxford
• Bristol   London •
Canterbury

Exeter •   Southampton •

Henry VII, King of England, Lord of Ireland, Prince of Wales

English Channel

0   50   100 miles
0   100   200 km

Channel Islands

FRANCE

The population of the British Isles, 1500 and 1750.

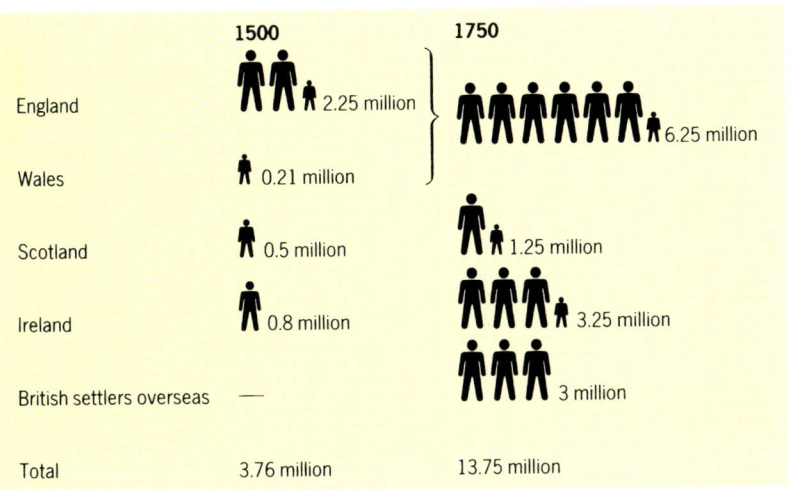

	1500	1750
England	2.25 million	6.25 million
Wales	0.21 million	
Scotland	0.5 million	1.25 million
Ireland	0.8 million	3.25 million
British settlers overseas	—	3 million
Total	3.76 million	13.75 million

Changes

There were many important changes between 1500 and 1750. Here are some of them:

There were more people in Britain.

The countries that had been England, Scotland, Wales and Ireland were now all part of one country – Great Britain.

The country changed from Roman Catholic in 1500 to Protestant in 1750.

In 1500 the country was run by the king. By 1750 the monarch was forced to rule the country with Parliament.